Building Networks and Servers Using BeagleBone

Set up and configure a local area network and file server by building your own home-based multimedia server

Bill Pretty

Glenn Vander Veer

BIRMINGHAM - MUMBAI

Building Networks and Servers Using BeagleBone

First published: May 2015

Production reference: 1250515

Published by Packt Publishing Ltd.
Livery Place
35 Livery Street
Birmingham B3 2PB, UK.

ISBN 978-1-78439-020-4

www.packtpub.com

Credits

Authors
Bill Pretty

Glenn Vander Veer

Reviewers
Raymond Boswel

Naoya Hashimoto

Jaime Soriano Pastor

Justin Smith

Norbert Varga

Commissioning Editor
Amarabha Banerjee

Acquisition Editor
Reshma Raman

Content Development Editor
Sweny Sukumaran

Technical Editor
Ryan Kochery

Copy Editor
Dipti Kapadia

Project Coordinator
Vijay Kushlani

Proofreaders
Stephen Copestake

Safis Editing

Indexer
Rekha Nair

Production Coordinator
Manu Joseph

Cover Work
Manu Joseph

About the Authors

Bill Pretty began his career in electronics in the early 80s with a small telecom start-up company that would eventually become a large multinational. He left this company to pursue a career in commercial aviation in northern Canada. Next, he joined the Ontario Center for Microelectronics, a provincially funded research and development center. Bill left this for a career in the military as a civilian contractor at what was then called Defense Research Establishment Ottawa. Thus began a career that was to span the next 25 years and continues until today.

Over the years, Bill acquired extensive knowledge in the field of technical security and started his own company in 2010. This company is called William Pretty Security Inc. and provides support in the form of research and development to various law enforcement and private security agencies.

Bill has published and presented a number of white papers on the subject of technical security. For a number of years, he was also a guest presenter at the Western Canada Technical Conference, a law enforcement-only conference held every year in western Canada. A selection of these papers is available for download from his website.

There are a number of people that I would like to thank, as without their support, this book would never have been completed. I would also like to thank my good friends at Packt Publishing for having patience and trust in me once again. Thanks to my partner in life, Donna, who never stopped believing in me.

Last but not least, I would like to thank my good friend and fellow code warrior Glenn "the flying Dutchman."

Glenn Vander Veer has been an embedded firmware developer for various microprocessors and microcontrollers for the past 20 years. He has been tinkering with electronics and all types of computers for over 30 years now. His interests lie in computer security, audio and video development, and tinkering with various operating systems. This is Glenn's first book, but definitely not his last.

I would like to thank Bill for bringing me in on this project.

About the Reviewers

Raymond Boswel is a software engineer who specializes in full-stack web development using Java, Linux, and various supporting technologies. He has a special fondness for writing code and enjoys learning new paradigms and languages. Raymond has also been a reviewer on *BeagleBone for Secret Agents* and *BeagleBone Home Automation*.

> I would like to thank all the wonderful people that I have been blessed to have in my life, for all the laughter, tears, and everything in between.

Naoya Hashimoto began his career as an infrastructure engineer, and he has experience in working with a data center, management service providers, and housing/hosting service providers. Recently, he has been working on multiple roles, such as service planning using open source software or third-party solutions, system integration on public clouds (mainly AWS), and system migrations from on-premises networks into public clouds. He has been a technical reviewer on *Mastering AWS Development*, *Building Networks and Servers Using BeagleBone*, *PostgreSQL Cookbook*, *Icinga Network Monitoring*, and *Building a Home Security System with BeagleBone*, all by Packt Publishing.

> Thanks for giving me the opportunity to join the review process of the book and to the author and coordinator for their contribution to this book. A huge thanks to one of my mentors, Mr. Abe at Info Circus, Inc., because I developed my career with his guidance in the first company where I worked and met him.

Jaime Soriano Pastor was born in Teruel, a small city in Spain. He has always been passionate about technology and sciences. While studying computer science at a university in his hometown, he had his first encounter with Linux and free software, which deeply shaped his career. Later on, he moved to Zaragoza to continue his studies. There, he worked for a couple of companies on different and interesting projects, from operative systems in embedded devices to the cloud, giving him a wide view on several fields of software development as well as some opportunities to travel around Europe. Currently, he lives in Madrid, and automation, configuration management, and continuous integration form a part of his daily work at a well-known technology company.

Justin Smith has a degree in computer science from Tennessee Technological University and is currently a systems and solutions integrator for an industrial IT firm in Nashville, Tennessee. He develops core software to interface with third-party hardware and software and has been introducing the software as modules into LabVIEW of late. Primarily a Java developer, Justin has been using open source tools to allow the code to be run from within LabVIEW.

Growing up around computers in the 80s, Justin has always known that he wanted to pursue a career in computing. Working as an intern in college and spending over a year in Central Mexico for his company, he realized all of the good that can be done by helping improve industrial processes (safety, quality, and efficiency). This made him decide that he wanted to continue working in industrial IT and automation, as he also feels that manufacturing and industry have yet to see the same technological revolutions as other business sectors through advances in companies such as Facebook and Google.

Justin has been working for Summit Management Systems, Inc of Nashville, Tennessee, for nearly 10 years. Summit Management Systems offers custom integration and process solutions worldwide for the industrial and manufacturing sector as well as several standalone software packages that aid in data acquisition from industrial devices and software to manufacture workflow management systems.

Norbert Varga has over 5 years experience in the software and hardware development industry, and he is responsible for embedded software development, hardware-software integration, and wireless telecommunication solutions at his current employer, BME-Infokom Innovátor Non-profit Ltd.

He has extensive experience in networking and hardware-software integration; he has engineered advanced systems, including wireless mesh networks and smart metering solutions. He also has a strong background in Linux system administration and software development.

Previously, Norbert worked as a software developer on various projects at the Budapest University of Technology and Economics (Department of Telecommunications), which is the most renowned technical university in Hungary. He played a key role throughout all the development processes, ranging from initial planning through implementation to testing and production support.

He has a personal blog, where he writes about his current projects (`http://nonoo.hu/`).

He has worked on several books by Packt Publishing, such as *BeagleBone for Secret Agents* and *Building a Home Security System with BeagleBone*.

www.PacktPub.com

Support files, eBooks, discount offers, and more

For support files and downloads related to your book, please visit www.PacktPub.com.

Did you know that Packt offers eBook versions of every book published, with PDF and ePub files available? You can upgrade to the eBook version at www.PacktPub.com and as a print book customer, you are entitled to a discount on the eBook copy. Get in touch with us at service@packtpub.com for more details.

At www.PacktPub.com, you can also read a collection of free technical articles, sign up for a range of free newsletters and receive exclusive discounts and offers on Packt books and eBooks.

https://www2.packtpub.com/books/subscription/packtlib

Do you need instant solutions to your IT questions? PacktLib is Packt's online digital book library. Here, you can search, access, and read Packt's entire library of books.

Why subscribe?

- Fully searchable across every book published by Packt
- Copy and paste, print, and bookmark content
- On demand and accessible via a web browser

Free access for Packt account holders

If you have an account with Packt at www.PacktPub.com, you can use this to access PacktLib today and view 9 entirely free books. Simply use your login credentials for immediate access.

This book is dedicated to the brave men and women from all corners of the civilized world who watch over us so that we may "sleep peacefully in our beds."

Thank you and stay safe.

-- Bill Pretty

Table of Contents

Preface

Learn how to build and configure your own network based on the BeagleBone. You will do this in a fun and informative way that will not only teach you networking skills but also result in an impressive project.

What this book covers

Chapter 1, *Installing Debian onto Your BeagleBone Black*, introduces how to install Debian onto your BeagleBone. There are two ways to boot the BeagleBone and run the OS.

Chapter 2, *Installing and Configuring Multimedia Server Software*, serves as an installation guide for the software that will be used to store the streamed video and to serve up both the audio and video files to any device on the network, either BB, computers, or tablets/phones.

Chapter 3, *Installing and Configuring Network Monitoring Software*, acts as an installation guide for the software that will be used to monitor the traffic on your local network.

Chapter 4, *Installing and Setting Up a BeagleBone RAID System*, acts as an installation guide for the software that will be used to create a RAID array out of the partitions that you will create on your USB-connected drives.

Chapter 5, *Streaming Videos*, will show you how to set up both live and recorded video streaming, using a web-based application.

Chapter 6, *Setting Up a Wireless Access Point*, shows you how to install and set up a wireless access point or WAP on your BeagleBone system.

What you need for this book

The following is a list of the suggested hardware for those of you who wish to build the entire system described in this book. Additional information has been outlined in the applicable chapters.

- **Two identical USB 2 memory sticks**: These should be at least 2 GB in size. The actual size depends on the amount of multimedia data you intend to store.

- **A Beagle Bone compatible USB 2 WiFi adapter**: There is a list of compatible adapters available at www.beaglebone.org.

- **A four-port USB 2 hub**: Depending on the output power of your WiFi adapter, a powered hub may be required.

- **An 8 GB, series 10, uSD card**: This is used to boot the root file system.

- **Win32DiskImager**: This is available with a search engine search. This will install the Debian image onto the uSD card.

Two memory sticks from the same manufacturer and same model number.

Who this book is for

This book is for beginners to intermediate readers who wish to learn more about how Linux networks are configured. You will learn this in a fun and informative way that will provide you with a finished product that you can enjoy and the skills to make improvements if you wish.

Conventions

In this book, you will find a number of text styles that distinguish between different kinds of information. Here are some examples of these styles and an explanation of their meaning.

Code words in text, database table names, folder names, filenames, file extensions, pathnames, dummy URLs, user input, and Twitter handles are shown as follows: "Once `fdisk` is running, enter p as the first command."

A block of code is set as follows:

```
### Wireless network name ###
interface=wlan0
### Set your bridge name ###
#bridge=br0
```

When we wish to draw your attention to a particular part of a code block, the relevant lines or items are set in bold:

```
#
DAEMON_CONF="/etc/hostapd/hostapd.conf" ß Add this line

# Additional daemon options to be appended to hostapd command:-
```

Any command-line input or output is written as follows:

```
sudo apt-get update
sudo apt-get upgrade
sudo apt-get dist-upgrade
```

New terms and **important words** are shown in bold. Words that you see on the screen, for example, in menus or dialog boxes, appear in the text like this: "It will be displayed as an **Open** network."

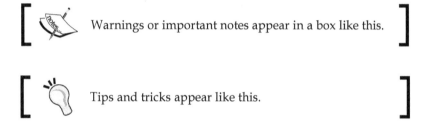

Warnings or important notes appear in a box like this.

Tips and tricks appear like this.

Reader feedback

Feedback from our readers is always welcome. Let us know what you think about this book—what you liked or disliked. Reader feedback is important for us as it helps us develop titles that you will really get the most out of.

To send us general feedback, simply e-mail feedback@packtpub.com, and mention the book's title in the subject of your message.

If there is a topic that you have expertise in and you are interested in either writing or contributing to a book, see our author guide at www.packtpub.com/authors.

Customer support

Now that you are the proud owner of a Packt book, we have a number of things to help you to get the most from your purchase.

Downloading the example code

You can download the example code files from your account at http://www.packtpub.com for all the Packt Publishing books you have purchased. If you purchased this book elsewhere, you can visit http://www.packtpub.com/support and register to have the files e-mailed directly to you.

Errata

Although we have taken every care to ensure the accuracy of our content, mistakes do happen. If you find a mistake in one of our books—maybe a mistake in the text or the code—we would be grateful if you could report this to us. By doing so, you can save other readers from frustration and help us improve subsequent versions of this book. If you find any errata, please report them by visiting http://www.packtpub.com/submit-errata, selecting your book, clicking on the **Errata Submission Form** link, and entering the details of your errata. Once your errata are verified, your submission will be accepted and the errata will be uploaded to our website or added to any list of existing errata under the Errata section of that title.

To view the previously submitted errata, go to https://www.packtpub.com/books/content/support and enter the name of the book in the search field. The required information will appear under the **Errata** section.

Piracy

Piracy of copyrighted material on the Internet is an ongoing problem across all media. At Packt, we take the protection of our copyright and licenses very seriously. If you come across any illegal copies of our works in any form on the Internet, please provide us with the location address or website name immediately so that we can pursue a remedy.

Please contact us at copyright@packtpub.com with a link to the suspected pirated material.

We appreciate your help in protecting our authors and our ability to bring you valuable content.

Questions

If you have a problem with any aspect of this book, you can contact us at questions@packtpub.com, and we will do our best to address the problem.

1

Installing Debian onto Your BeagleBone Black

In this chapter, you will learn how to install Debian onto your BeagleBone. There are two ways to boot the BeagleBone and run the OS: the first way is to run off the microSD card, and the second is to run off the internal eMMC (flash). BeagleBone has 4 GB of onboard flash, which is not expandable. It is recommended that the microSD be used so that there is ample room left for you to install other programs that will be needed later in the book, and this is what will be shown in this chapter. In order to install the OS, you require a microSD card (an 8 GB card will be fine), an SD card reader (which most laptops have built-in), and the Windows program Win32 DiskImager. This program will write the actual OS image to the SD card, which the BeagleBone will boot from. An archival program, such as WinRAR or 7-Zip, is also needed to extract the OS image from the downloaded archive.

Setting up to install Debian

At this point, you should install Win32 DiskImager and the archival program. This will be used to write the Debian image on the SD card. The archive for the disk image is located at `http://beagleboard.org/latest-images` and `http://debian.beagleboard.org/images/bone-debian-7.8-lxde-4gb-armhf-2015-03-01-4gb.img.xz`.

In order to start the installation, perform the following steps:

1. Extract the files from this archive and run **Win32 Disk Imager**. If you are using Windows 7 or higher, you will have to run the program as an administrator in order to write the Debian image to the SD card.

2. Select the extracted image file using the blue-colored folder icon, and make sure that the device selected to be written to (F:\ in the following picture) is your SD card.

3. Click on write and the image will be written to the SD card, as shown in the following screenshot:

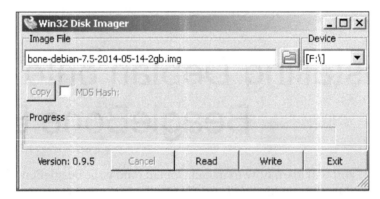

4. Once the image is written to the SD card, remove the card from the PC and insert it into the SD card slot on the BeagleBone.

The following image shows the BeagleBone board with HDMI, Ethernet, and USB installed and an SD card inserted:

At this point, the board is ready to be powered up and to run Debian. The USB cable may not have enough capacity to power the BeagleBone board, so it is strongly suggested that the board be powered by a 5-volt DC power cube with a current output of 2 amps. This will provide sufficient power to the board. Turn on the power to the board. If the board does not power up, press *S3* to enable the power. *S3* is located directly above the Ethernet connection. After about a minute, your screen should display a login prompt. If this does not happen, power off the board and hold down the boot button (located near the top-right corner of the board, close to the SD card); then apply power to the board and don't release the boot button until the user LEDs begin to flicker.

The following screenshot shows the display that you will get after you log in for the first time:

In order to login, the username is debian and the password is temppwd. The next thing that needs to be done is to get all the updates that are available, and then the image should be resized in order to use the entire 8 GB of the SD card. In order to update, the following commands should be run:

```
sudo apt-get update
sudo apt-get upgrade
sudo apt-get dist-upgrade
```

All of these three commands can be run at the same time by inserting && between each command. After the update is completed, reboot the board (sudo reboot) and relogin. At this point, the image will be resized to use the entire size of the SD card.

Before the resizing operation, run the following command to show how much of the SD is being used:

```
df -h
```

The following screenshot shows the output of the df -h command:

```
Filesystem      Size  Used Avail Use% Mounted on
/dev/mmcblk0p2  1.8G  396M  1.3G  24% /
devtmpfs        248M  4.0K  248M   1% /dev
none             50M  248K   50M   1% /run
none            5.0M     0  5.0M   0% /run/lock
none            248M     0  248M   0% /run/shm
/dev/mmcblk0p1 1004K  472K  532K  48% /boot/uboot
```

Using the SD card before the resizing operation

First, list the volumes that are available on the SD card by running the following command:

ls -l /dev/mmcblk*

The output will show all the volumes, as shown in the following screenshot. The volume that will be modified is the first volume in the list, /dev/mmcblk0. This is because mmcblk0 refers to the SD card.

A list of all the available volumes is shown in this screenshot.

```
brw-rw---- 1 root disk 179,  0 Jun 25 14:54 /dev/mmcblk0
brw-rw---- 1 root disk 179,  1 Jun 25 14:54 /dev/mmcblk0p1
brw-rw---- 1 root disk 179,  2 Jun 25 14:54 /dev/mmcblk0p2
brw-rw---- 1 root disk 179,  8 Jun 25 14:54 /dev/mmcblk1
brw-rw---- 1 root disk 179, 16 Jun 25 14:54 /dev/mmcblk1boot0
brw-rw---- 1 root disk 179, 24 Jun 25 14:54 /dev/mmcblk1boot1
brw-rw---- 1 root disk 179,  9 Jun 25 14:54 /dev/mmcblk1p1
brw-rw---- 1 root disk 179, 10 Jun 25 14:54 /dev/mmcblk1p2
                  :~$ sudo fdisk /dev/mmcblk0
Command (m for help):
```

At this point, the superuser should be logged in to complete the disk resizing, by executing the following command:

sudo su

Again, the password is temppwd. Once the superuser is active, run fdisk on the first volume with the following command (also shown in the preceding screenshot):

fdisk /dev/mmcblk0

Once fdisk is running, enter p as the first command. This will display the partition information of the SD. The resizing operation will delete the empty partitions and expand the primary partition to use the entire SD.

First, press d for delete and then press 2 for partition 2. Next, press n for new, p for primary, and 2 for partition 2. Specify the start and end sectors for the new partition – just select the default values by pressing *Enter*. In fact, outside the first n, they are all default choices and pressing *Enter* alone to confirm the choice is all that is needed. Select w to commit the changes to the SD card. Notice that the partition table in this example was "busy," so a reboot is needed for the changes to be reflected. Reboot by entering sudo reboot from the terminal command line, and re-login to update the changes for the next step of resizing the filesystem.

As we can see in the following image, the resized partition is ready to have the file system resized onto it.

```
root@beaglebone:~# fdisk /dev/mmcblk0

Command (m for help): p

Disk /dev/mmcblk0: 8035 MB, 8035237888 bytes
4 heads, 16 sectors/track, 245216 cylinders, total 15693824 sectors
Units = sectors of 1 * 512 = 512 bytes
Sector size (logical/physical): 512 bytes / 512 bytes
I/O size (minimum/optimal): 512 bytes / 512 bytes
Disk identifier: 0x00000000

        Device Boot      Start         End      Blocks   Id  System
/dev/mmcblk0p1   *        2048      198655       98304    e  W95 FAT16 (LBA)
/dev/mmcblk0p2          198656     7577599     3689472   83  Linux

Command (m for help): d
Partition number (1-4): 2

Command (m for help): n
Partition type:
   p   primary (1 primary, 0 extended, 3 free)
   e   extended
Select (default p): p
Partition number (1-4, default 2): 2
First sector (198656-15693823, default 198656):
Using default value 198656
Last sector, +sectors or +size{K,M,G} (198656-15693823, default 15693823):
Using default value 15693823

Command (m for help): w
The partition table has been altered!

Calling ioctl() to re-read partition table.

WARNING: Re-reading the partition table failed with error 16: Device or resource
 busy.
The kernel still uses the old table. The new table will be used at
the next reboot or after you run partprobe(8) or kpartx(8)
Syncing disks.
```

Now the file system is ready to be resized. This will take only one command, as follows:

```
resize2fs /dev/mmcblk0p2
```

After this command, the SD card will have all its space available to the OS. Running another df -h command will confirm that the new disk size is now much more than 2 GB.

The following screenshot shows the new file system on the SD card, which resulted from running the resize2fs command:

```
root@beaglebone:~# sudo resize2fs /dev/mmcblk0p2
resize2fs 1.42.5 (29-Jul-2012)
Filesystem at /dev/mmcblk0p2 is mounted on /; on-line resizing required
old_desc_blocks = 1, new_desc_blocks = 1
The filesystem on /dev/mmcblk0p2 is now 1936896 blocks long.

root@beaglebone:~# df -h
Filesystem        Size  Used Avail Use% Mounted on
rootfs            7.3G  1.8G  5.2G  26% /
udev              10M     0   10M   0% /dev
tmpfs            100M  648K   99M   1% /run
/dev/mmcblk0p2    7.3G  1.8G  5.2G  26% /
tmpfs            249M     0  249M   0% /dev/shm
tmpfs            249M     0  249M   0% /sys/fs/cgroup
tmpfs            100M     0  100M   0% /run/user
tmpfs            5.0M     0  5.0M   0% /run/lock
/dev/mmcblk1p1    96M    72M   25M  75% /media/boot
/dev/mmcblk0p1    96M    64M   33M  67% /media/BEAGLEBONE
/dev/mmcblk1p2    3.4G  1.5G  1.8G  45% /media/rootfs
root@beaglebone:~# []
```

Installing Tightvnc

In order to remotely access the BeagleBone, the **Tightvnc** server needs to be installed with the following command:

```
sudo apt-get install tightvncserver
```

Once the server is installed, it needs to be set up as follows:

```
tightvncserver :1
```

This will then ask for a password to access the desktop. Enter a password and verify it. This will be the password used to login to the BeagleBone with the VNC remote viewing client. If a remote connection is needed, to view what is happening on the BeagleBone, a separate password can be entered.

```
root@beaglebone:~# tightvncserver :1

You will require a password to access your desktops.

Password:
Verify:
Would you like to enter a view-only password (y/n)? n
xauth:  file /root/.Xauthority does not exist

New 'X' desktop is beaglebone:1

Creating default startup script /root/.vnc/xstartup
Starting applications specified in /root/.vnc/xstartup
Log file is /root/.vnc/beaglebone:1.log
```

After the server is set up, reboot and re-login. Open a terminal and enter the following command to get the IP address of the BeagleBone:

`ifconfig`

This will be needed on the remote PC to access the system.

```
root@beaglebone:~# ifconfig
eth0      Link encap:Ethernet  HWaddr 1c:ba:8c:96:51:41
          inet addr:192.168.1.13  Bcast:192.168.1.255  Mask:255.255.255.0
          inet6 addr: fe80::1eba:8cff:fe96:5141/64 Scope:Link
          UP BROADCAST RUNNING MULTICAST  MTU:1500  Metric:1
          RX packets:414 errors:0 dropped:3 overruns:0 frame:0
          TX packets:160 errors:0 dropped:0 overruns:0 carrier:0
          collisions:0 txqueuelen:1000
          RX bytes:71155 (69.4 KiB)  TX bytes:23851 (23.2 KiB)
          Interrupt:40

lo        Link encap:Local Loopback
          inet addr:127.0.0.1  Mask:255.0.0.0
          inet6 addr: ::1/128 Scope:Host
          UP LOOPBACK RUNNING  MTU:65536  Metric:1
          RX packets:0 errors:0 dropped:0 overruns:0 frame:0
          TX packets:0 errors:0 dropped:0 overruns:0 carrier:0
          collisions:0 txqueuelen:0
          RX bytes:0 (0.0 B)  TX bytes:0 (0.0 B)

usb0      Link encap:Ethernet  HWaddr 62:19:c1:67:36:05
          inet addr:192.168.7.2  Bcast:192.168.7.3  Mask:255.255.255.252
          UP BROADCAST MULTICAST  MTU:1500  Metric:1
          RX packets:0 errors:0 dropped:0 overruns:0 frame:0
          TX packets:0 errors:0 dropped:0 overruns:0 carrier:0
          collisions:0 txqueuelen:1000
          RX bytes:0 (0.0 B)  TX bytes:0 (0.0 B)
```

Run the VNC server in order to allow the BeagleBone to start accepting remote connections with the `tightvncserver :1` command.

On the remote computer, a VNC viewer should be installed. There are many options to choose from, which will work. In the remote address, enter the BeagleBone's IP address and add the `:1` at the end and connect to the BeagleBone.

When you run the VNC viewer, you will see a "connection" screen similar to the one shown in the following screenshot:

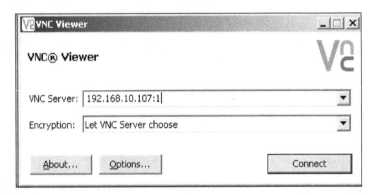

The default encryption method is to let VNC choose, so just go with the default. The next window that pops up will be the login window, where you have to enter the password that you were prompted for when you installed the VNC Server, as shown in the following screenshot:

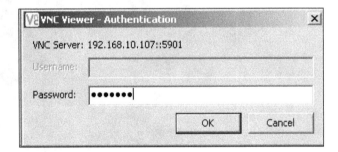

Downloading the example code

You can download the example code files from your account at `http://www.packtpub.com` for all the Packt Publishing books you have purchased. If you purchased this book elsewhere, you can visit `http://www.packtpub.com/support` and register to have the files e-mailed directly to you.

Running the Cloud9 IDE

Fortunately for us, the good folks who maintain the Debian image files have included the Cloud9 IDE in the standard image. For those of you who don't know what an IDE is, the letters stand for **Integrated Development Environment**. Cloud9 allows you to write and debug various types of source code. In order to access Cloud9, you have to simply enter the IP address of the BeagleBone in your favorite web browser followed by :3000, because Cloud9 uses port 3000.

Summary

In this chapter, the BeagleBone was set up to run Debian on a resized SD card. The image was also updated to get the latest upgrades available. Then, the LXDE desktop environment was installed. Finally, the Cloud9 IDE was set up and run. Now, the BeagleBone is ready to build the applications needed to control the devices discussed in the later chapters. In the next chapter, we will talk about the software that will be used to store streamed video, and serve up both audio and video files to any device on the network.

2
Installing and Configuring Multimedia Server Software

This chapter will serve as an installation guide for the software that will be used to store streamed videos and to serve up both the audio and video files to any device on the network, either BB or computers or tablets/phones. However, first some "housekeeping" needs to be done to the packages that were installed in the last chapter. For this, we will do the following:

- Set up the BeagleBone to have a static IP.

- Start the VNC server as soon as the BeagleBone is powered on.

- Set the time and date to their proper values and to automatically update via NTP time servers.

- After the housekeeping, download and set up Samba for the BeagleBone. Samba is going to be used because it is easy to configure and maintain. This will be used to load the MP3 files into their proper shared directory and for the video streaming to store the video files for playback later.

- Download and set up the DLNA server software for the BeagleBone. This will allow the audio and video files to be browsed and *served* to other devices on the network.

Setting up a static IP on the BeagleBone

First, display the contents of the /etc/network/interfaces file. Run the
following command:

`cat /etc/network/interfaces`

If the board is configured to use DHCP services (the default configuration),
dhcp appears at the end of the following line:

`iface eth0 inet dhcp`

If the board is configured to use static IP settings, static appears at the end of the
line instead of dhcp.

The following screenshot shows the output of the cat /etc/network/interfaces
command:

```
# interfaces(5) file used by ifup(8) and ifdown(8)

# loopback network interface
auto lo
iface lo inet loopback

# primary network interface
auto eth0
iface eth0 inet dhcp
#hwaddress ether DE:AD:BE:EF:CA:FE

# wireless network interface
#auto wlan0
#iface wlan0 inet dhcp
#    wpa-ssid "my_wifi_name"
#    wpa-psk  "my_wifi_pass"
```

Now, create a backup of the /etc/network/interfaces file by running the
following command:

`sudo cp /etc/network/interfaces /etc/network/interfaces.backup`

Now, edit the interfaces file with nano, as follows:

`iface eth0 inet dhcp`

Change the preceding command line to this:

```
iface eth0 inet static
```

```
root@beaglebone:~# cat /etc/network/interfaces
# This file describes the network interfaces available on your system
# and how to activate them. For more information, see interfaces(5).

# The loopback network interface
auto lo
iface lo inet loopback

# The primary network interface
auto eth0
#iface eth0 inet dhcp
iface eth0 inet static
address 192.168.10.127
netmask 255.255.255.0
gateway 192.168.10.1

# Example to keep MAC address between reboots
#hwaddress ether DE:AD:BE:EF:CA:FE

# The secondary network interface
#auto eth1
#iface eth1 inet dhcp

# WiFi Example
auto wlan0
iface wlan0 inet static
    wpa-ssid "Multimedia Server"
#   wpa-psk  "password"
address 192.168.4.1
network 192.168.4.0
netmask 255.255.255.0
broadcast 192.168.4.255

# Ethernet/RNDIS gadget (g_ether)
# ... or on host side, usbnet and random hwaddr
# Note on some boards, usb0 is automaticly setup with an init script
iface usb0 inet static
    address 192.168.7.2
    netmask 255.255.255.0
    network 192.168.7.0
    gateway 192.168.7.1
root@beaglebone:~#
```

Now, enter the following command in the terminal:

```
ifconfig
```

On the command line, you will see something similar to what is shown in the following screenshot:

```
192.168.10.127 - PuTTY                                                    _ □ X
root@beaglebone:~# ifconfig
eth0      Link encap:Ethernet  HWaddr 1c:ba:8c:e1:85:5e
          inet addr:192.168.10.127  Bcast:192.168.10.255  Mask:255.255.255.0
          inet6 addr: fe80::1eba:8cff:fee1:855e/64 Scope:Link
          UP BROADCAST RUNNING MULTICAST  MTU:1500  Metric:1
          RX packets:809 errors:0 dropped:0 overruns:0 frame:0
          TX packets:514 errors:0 dropped:0 overruns:0 carrier:0
          collisions:0 txqueuelen:1000
          RX bytes:187583 (183.1 KiB)  TX bytes:55458 (54.1 KiB)
          Interrupt:40

lo        Link encap:Local Loopback
          inet addr:127.0.0.1  Mask:255.0.0.0
          inet6 addr: ::1/128 Scope:Host
          UP LOOPBACK RUNNING  MTU:65536  Metric:1
          RX packets:5 errors:0 dropped:0 overruns:0 frame:0
          TX packets:5 errors:0 dropped:0 overruns:0 carrier:0
          collisions:0 txqueuelen:0
          RX bytes:319 (319.0 B)  TX bytes:319 (319.0 B)

mon.wlan0 Link encap:UNSPEC  HWaddr E0-CB-4E-A6-58-EC-00-00-00-00-00-00-00-00-00-00
          UP BROADCAST RUNNING MULTICAST  MTU:1500  Metric:1
          RX packets:700 errors:0 dropped:0 overruns:0 frame:0
          TX packets:0 errors:0 dropped:0 overruns:0 carrier:0
          collisions:0 txqueuelen:1000
          RX bytes:60488 (59.0 KiB)  TX bytes:0 (0.0 B)

usb0      Link encap:Ethernet  HWaddr 72:80:d1:d9:e2:06
          inet addr:192.168.7.2  Bcast:192.168.7.3  Mask:255.255.255.252
          UP BROADCAST MULTICAST  MTU:1500  Metric:1
          RX packets:0 errors:0 dropped:0 overruns:0 frame:0
          TX packets:0 errors:0 dropped:0 overruns:0 carrier:0
          collisions:0 txqueuelen:1000
          RX bytes:0 (0.0 B)  TX bytes:0 (0.0 B)

wlan0     Link encap:Ethernet  HWaddr e0:cb:4e:a6:58:ec
          inet addr:192.168.4.1  Bcast:192.168.4.255  Mask:255.255.255.0
          inet6 addr: fe80::e2cb:4eff:fea6:58ec/64 Scope:Link
          UP BROADCAST RUNNING MULTICAST  MTU:1500  Metric:1
          RX packets:0 errors:0 dropped:0 overruns:0 frame:0
          TX packets:61 errors:0 dropped:0 overruns:0 carrier:0
          collisions:0 txqueuelen:1000
          RX bytes:0 (0.0 B)  TX bytes:10014 (9.7 KiB)

root@beaglebone:~# ▋
```

Starting the VNC server

To start the VNC server after booting and logging in, we just SSH to the multimedia server and enter the following command:

```
tightvncserver
```

The terminal will display the following response:

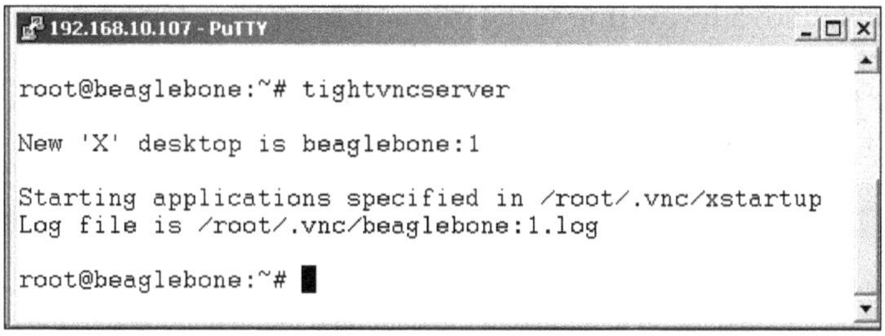

```
192.168.10.107 - PuTTY                                    _ | □ | x |
root@beaglebone:~# tightvncserver

New 'X' desktop is beaglebone:1

Starting applications specified in /root/.vnc/xstartup
Log file is /root/.vnc/beaglebone:1.log

root@beaglebone:~# █
```

You can now access the multimedia server's desktop from your PC or Mac.

Installing NTP

Every time the board is powered, the clock is reset. This can be inconvenient when using a source code repository; therefore, the **Network Time Protocol** (**NTP**) will be installed and set up so that the board updates to the current time and date on power up. To install NTP, run the following command:

```
sudo apt-get install ntp
```

Here's the output of the NTP install command:

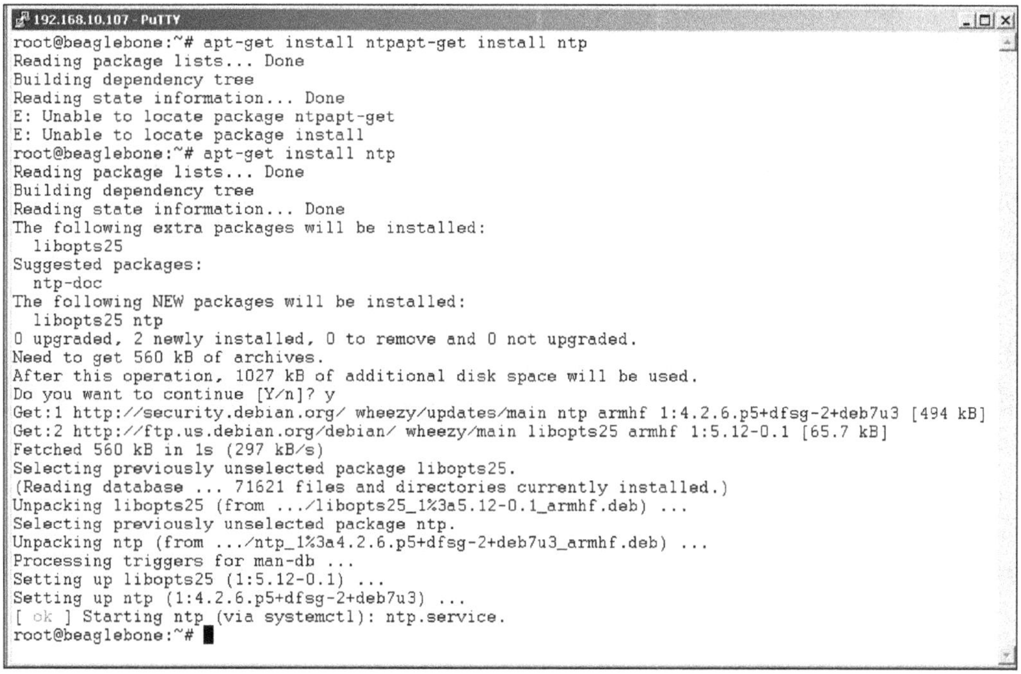

```
192.168.10.107 - PuTTY                                                                    _ | □ | x |
root@beaglebone:~# apt-get install ntpapt-get install ntp
Reading package lists... Done
Building dependency tree
Reading state information... Done
E: Unable to locate package ntpapt-get
E: Unable to locate package install
root@beaglebone:~# apt-get install ntp
Reading package lists... Done
Building dependency tree
Reading state information... Done
The following extra packages will be installed:
  libopts25
Suggested packages:
  ntp-doc
The following NEW packages will be installed:
  libopts25 ntp
0 upgraded, 2 newly installed, 0 to remove and 0 not upgraded.
Need to get 560 kB of archives.
After this operation, 1027 kB of additional disk space will be used.
Do you want to continue [Y/n]? y
Get:1 http://security.debian.org/ wheezy/updates/main ntp armhf 1:4.2.6.p5+dfsg-2+deb7u3 [494 kB]
Get:2 http://ftp.us.debian.org/debian/ wheezy/main libopts25 armhf 1:5.12-0.1 [65.7 kB]
Fetched 560 kB in 1s (297 kB/s)
Selecting previously unselected package libopts25.
(Reading database ... 71621 files and directories currently installed.)
Unpacking libopts25 (from .../libopts25_1%3a5.12-0.1_armhf.deb) ...
Selecting previously unselected package ntp.
Unpacking ntp (from .../ntp_1%3a4.2.6.p5+dfsg-2+deb7u3_armhf.deb) ...
Processing triggers for man-db ...
Setting up libopts25 (1:5.12-0.1) ...
Setting up ntp (1:4.2.6.p5+dfsg-2+deb7u3) ...
[ ok ] Starting ntp (via systemctl): ntp.service.
root@beaglebone:~# █
```

Setting the local time zone

Once NTP is installed, a local time server should be set to offload the requests from global time servers. This is done by editing the /etc/ntp.conf file and replacing one or more of the default servers with a local time server that can be found via a web search. The following is an example ntp.conf file:

```
 192.168.10.127 - PuTTY

root@beaglebone:/etc# cat ntp.conf
# /etc/ntp.conf, configuration for ntpd; see ntp.conf(5) for help

driftfile /var/lib/ntp/ntp.drift


# Enable this if you want statistics to be logged.
#statsdir /var/log/ntpstats/

statistics loopstats peerstats clockstats
filegen loopstats file loopstats type day enable
filegen peerstats file peerstats type day enable
filegen clockstats file clockstats type day enable


# You do need to talk to an NTP server or two (or three).
#server ntp.your-provider.example

# pool.ntp.org maps to about 1000 low-stratum NTP servers.  Your server will
# pick a different set every time it starts up.  Please consider joining the
# pool: <http://www.pool.ntp.org/join.html>
server 0.debian.pool.ntp.org iburst
server 1.debian.pool.ntp.org iburst
server 2.debian.pool.ntp.org iburst
server 3.debian.pool.ntp.org iburst
```

The local time zone should be set as well, and there are two ways of achieving this. First, by running this command:

```
sudo dpkg-reconfigure tzdata
```

This will set the time zone, or by making a symbolic link to the proper time zone settings file, which is located in /usr/share/zoneinfo.

This is what the time zone data for Canada looks like:

```
192.168.10.127 - PuTTY                                                    _ |□| x|
root@beaglebone:/usr/share/zoneinfo/Canada# ls -l
total 0
lrwxrwxrwx 1 root root 24 Feb  1 05:44 Atlantic -> ../posix/SystemV/AST4ADT
lrwxrwxrwx 1 root root 23 Feb  1 05:44 Central -> ../posix/Canada/Central
lrwxrwxrwx 1 root root 21 Feb  1 05:44 East-Saskatchewan -> ../posix/SystemV/CST
lrwxrwxrwx 1 root root 23 Feb  1 05:44 Eastern -> ../posix/Canada/Eastern
lrwxrwxrwx 1 root root 24 Feb  1 05:44 Mountain -> ../posix/Canada/Mountain
lrwxrwxrwx 1 root root 28 Feb  1 05:44 Newfoundland -> ../posix/Canada/Newfoundl
lrwxrwxrwx 1 root root 23 Feb  1 05:44 Pacific -> ../posix/Canada/Pacific
lrwxrwxrwx 1 root root 21 Feb  1 05:44 Saskatchewan -> ../posix/SystemV/CST6
lrwxrwxrwx 1 root root 21 Feb  1 05:44 Yukon -> ../posix/Canada/Yukon
root@beaglebone:/usr/share/zoneinfo/Canada# ▌
```

To set the local time zone, first remove the default `localtime` file with the following command:

```
sudo rm /etc/localtime
```

Then, create a link to the `localtime` file that is closest to the time zone that you are in, with the following command:

```
sudo ln -s /usr/share/zoneinfo/Canada/Eastern /etc/localtime
```

This finishes up the housekeeping that needs to be done. Reboot the BeagleBone to get the new setup.

Installing and configuring Samba

Samba is a very convenient application to have running for a home media server, as it allows easy access to files from other computers on the local network. Here, Samba is configured to be used with authentication and authorization. In other words, a username and password must be used in order to access Samba's shared folders from any network connection. In order to access the folders, they will be *mapped* to a local drive on the non-BeagleBone system. Then, the Samba share will appear as a local drive on the non-BeagleBone system, even though it is actually a folder on the BeagleBone. On the Windows operating system, this is easily accomplished by the **map network drive** option. This option is available by right-clicking on the shared folder in a **File Explorer** window.

To install samba, use the following command:

```
sudo apt-get install samba
```

Sometimes, there are extra packages that need to be installed in addition to the package you want to install. After reading the details of these packages, select Y to continue, as shown in the following screenshot:

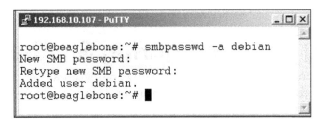

```
192.168.10.107 - PuTTY                                          _ □ ×
root@beaglebone:~# apt-get install samba
Reading package lists... Done
Building dependency tree
Reading state information... Done
The following extra packages will be installed:
  samba-common samba-common-bin tdb-tools
Suggested packages:
  openbsd-inetd inet-superserver smbldap-tools ldb-tools ctdb
The following NEW packages will be installed:
  samba samba-common samba-common-bin tdb-tools
0 upgraded, 4 newly installed, 0 to remove and 0 not upgraded.
Need to get 6359 kB of archives.
After this operation, 29.2 MB of additional disk space will be used.
Do you want to continue [Y/n]? ▮
```

Now, a password is needed to access the server from other remote clients. The user will be the default user (debian). To set the password, run the following command:

```
sudo smbpasswd -a debian
```

The following screenshot shows how to set the **SMB password** for the debian user:

```
192.168.10.107 - PuTTY                            _ □ ×
root@beaglebone:~# smbpasswd -a debian
New SMB password:
Retype new SMB password:
Added user debian.
root@beaglebone:~# ▮
```

Now, /etc/samba/smb.conf will be changed to increase security and remove some unnecessary settings.

First, ensure that the Samba shares can only be accessed by devices on the local network by restricting the IP addresses that Samba will respond to. This is done by adding the following lines in the #### Networking #### section:

```
hosts allow = 127.0.0.1 192.168.1.0/24
hosts deny = 0.0.0.0/0
```

Make sure that the `hosts allow` line reflects your local network settings. Your local subnet may be different from the `X.X.1.0/24`, as shown in the previous command.

Next, make sure that the following line is present and uncommented in the `######` `Authentication ######` section:

`security = user`

This will ensure that the only people who can access Samba shares are those who have a valid Debian account on the BeagleBone.

Now, you need to comment out any of the lines pertaining to `printers` because the BeagleBone is not going to be attached to any.

Anything in the `; [printers]` section should be commented out with a `";"`.

Later on in *Chapter 4, Installing and Setting Up a BeagleBone RAID System*, when the external **RAID array** is attached, the `smb.conf` file will need to be edited and the Raid array will need to be entered in to allow access over Samba.

This entry will then become the "mapping" point on the non-BeagleBone system and will appear as a local drive. This will be where the video, audio, and pictures will be stored.

To do this, the following lines are entered:

```
#Share for the Raid array
[media]
  Comment= Raid array connected to BeagleBone
  path = /media/<Raid mount point>
  read only = no
  browseable = yes
  valid users = <debian>
```

Now, enter the `reboot` command to restart Linux.

Installing the DLNA server

Digital Living Network Alliance (**DLNA**), which is a group of organizations that have created an industry-wide standard, enables all DLNA devices to share media over a home network. Once a device is connected to a DLNA server, media content can be accessed with minimum hassle so that movies, music, or digital photos are available to be played on game consoles, tablets, mobile phones, and televisions.

This content will be loaded by remote machines using the Samba shares that have been mapped as part of their filesystem. Once the network and server is set up, content can be added and viewed at anytime, anywhere on the local network.

Now, the DLNA server will be installed with the following command:

```
sudo apt-get install minidlna
```

Installing the DLNA server will have extra packages that need to be installed in addition to the package you want to install. After reading the details of these packages, select y to continue, as shown in the following screenshot:

```
root@beaglebone:~# apt-get install minidlna
Reading package lists... Done
Building dependency tree
Reading state information... Done
The following NEW packages will be installed:
  minidlna
0 upgraded, 1 newly installed, 0 to remove and 0 not upgraded.
Need to get 137 kB of archives.
After this operation, 285 kB of additional disk space will be used.
Get:1 http://ftp.us.debian.org/debian/ wheezy/main minidlna armhf 1.0.24+dfsg-1
[137 kB]
Fetched 137 kB in 2s (51.1 kB/s)
Selecting previously unselected package minidlna.
(Reading database ... 71792 files and directories currently installed.)
Unpacking minidlna (from .../minidlna_1.0.24+dfsg-1_armhf.deb) ...
Processing triggers for man-db ...
Setting up minidlna (1.0.24+dfsg-1) ...
[ ok ] Starting minidlna (via systemctl): minidlna.service.
root@beaglebone:~#
```

Once the server is installed, its settings can be modified by editing /etc/minidlna. conf. Once again, the entries in this file will be done later on when the external Raid array is set up and attached. This last section of the chapter should be bookmarked so that it can be easily found when that time comes.

Edit the file to add the media directories; at the end, it will have the uncommented lines, which might look like this:

```
$ grep -o "^[a-z].*" /etc/minidlna.conf
port=8200
media_dir=V,/home/user/media/Movies
media_dir=A,/home/user/media/Music
media_dir=P,/home/user/media/Pictures
friendly_name=BeagleBone DLNA Server
```

```
album_art_names=Cover.jpg/cover.jpg/AlbumArtSmall.jpg/albumartsmall.jpg/
AlbumArt.jpg/albumart.jpg/Album.jpg/album.jpg/Folder.jpg/folder.jpg/
Thumb.jpg/thumb.jpg
inotify=yes
enable_tivo=no
strict_dlna=no
notify_interval=900
serial=12345678
model_number=1
```

The `media` directory entries will be the entries that are changed to match the mounted directories on the Raid array.

After saving the `.conf` file, the DLNA server needs to be forced into rescanning the new folder locations for media files. This is done with the following command:

```
sudo /etc/init.d/minidlna force-reload
```

The following screenshot shows the `force-reload` command to refresh the server:

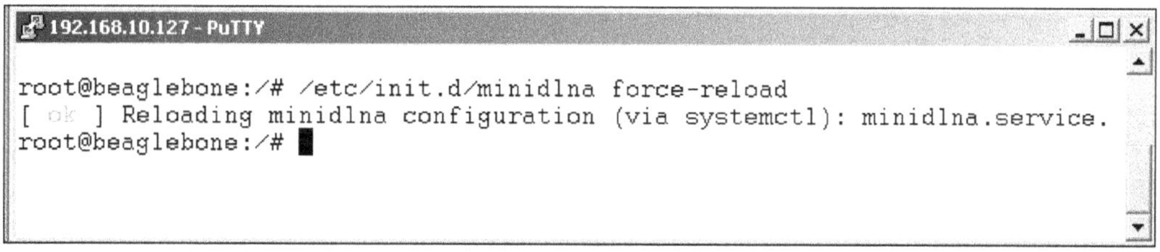

Now, the DLNA server is running and can be browsed with any DLNA-aware device or media player. All that is needed now is the Raid array to store the media files and the content to fill up the array.

Here's the BeagleBone displayed in **Windows Media Player**:

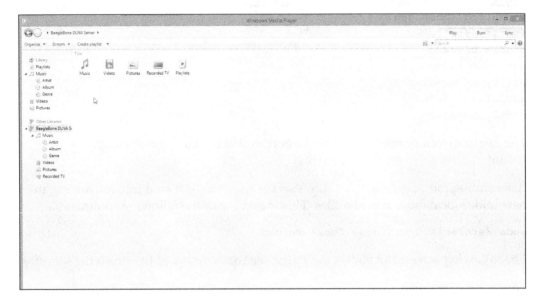

Summary

In this chapter, the BeagleBone was set up to update the time and date via NTP. It was also configured to automatically start the VNC server so that an external keyboard, mouse, and display will not be needed to control the BeagleBone. Next, Samba was installed to allow access to the yet to be connected Raid array, and a DLNA server was installed in order to serve up audio, video, and pictures to the properly authenticated user.

In the next chapter, we will talk about the software needed to secure the network from any unauthorized use.

3
Installing and Configuring Network Monitoring Software

This chapter will serve as an installation guide for the software that will be used to monitor the traffic on your local network. These utilities can help determine which devices on your network are hogging the bandwidth, which slows down the network for other devices on your network. Here are the topics that we are going to cover in this chapter:

- Installing **traceroute** and **My Trace Route** (MTR or Matt's Traceroute): These utilities will give you a real-time view of the connection between one node and another

- Installing **Nmap**: This utility is a network scanner that can list all the hosts on your network and all the services available on those hosts

- Installing **iptraf-ng**: This utility gathers various network traffic information and statistics

Installing Traceroute

Traceroute is a tool that can show the path from one node on a network to another. This can help determine the ideal placement of a router to maximize wireless bandwidth in order to stream music and videos from the BeagleBone server to remote devices. Traceroute can be installed with the following command:

```
apt-get install traceroute
```

```
root@beaglebone:~# apt-get install mtr
Reading package lists... Done
Building dependency tree
Reading state information... Done
The following NEW packages will be installed:
  mtr
0 upgraded, 1 newly installed, 0 to remove and 1 not upgraded.
Need to get 57.4 kB of archives.
After this operation, 130 kB of additional disk space will be used.
Get:1 http://ftp.us.debian.org/debian/ wheezy/main mtr armhf 0.82-3 [57.4 kB]
Fetched 57.4 kB in 0s (106 kB/s)
Selecting previously unselected package mtr.
(Reading database ... 59626 files and directories currently installed.)
Unpacking mtr (from .../archives/mtr_0.82-3_armhf.deb) ...
Processing triggers for man-db ...
Setting up mtr (0.82-3) ...
```

Once Traceroute is installed, it can be run to find the path from the BeagleBone to any server anywhere in the world. For example, here's the route from my BeagelBone to the Canadian Google servers:

```
root@beaglebone:~# traceroute google.ca
traceroute to google.ca (74.125.225.23), 30 hops max, 60 byte packets
 1  WNDR4500v2.local (192.168.1.1)  1.936 ms  2.915 ms  2.872 ms
 2  10.149.206.1 (10.149.206.1)  15.335 ms  17.319 ms  17.232 ms
 3  dtr01bxtrmn-tge-0-0-0-3.bxtr.mn.charter.com (96.34.26.56)  17.207 ms  16.719 ms  28.205 ms
 4  dtr01alxnmn-tge-0-1-0-1.alxn.mn.charter.com (96.34.27.90)  31.484 ms dtr01alxnmn-tge-0-1-0-0.alxn.
mn.charter.com (96.34.27.20)  31.422 ms dtr01alxnmn-tge-0-1-0-1.alxn.mn.charter.com (96.34.27.90)  31.
236 ms
 5  dtr02stcdmn-tge-0-5-0-10.stcd.mn.charter.com (96.34.27.46)  31.850 ms  32.602 ms  31.379 ms
 6  crr02stcdmn-bue-6.stcd.mn.charter.com (96.34.27.108)  32.092 ms  17.880 ms  43.844 ms
 7  bbr01stcdmn-bue-3.stcd.mn.charter.com (96.34.2.136)  43.599 ms  23.363 ms  23.721 ms
 8  bbr02chcgil-bue-1.chcg.il.charter.com (96.34.1.149)  38.412 ms  38.351 ms  37.565 ms
 9  prr01chcgil-bue-4.chcg.il.charter.com (96.34.3.11)  37.084 ms  36.368 ms  41.885 ms
10  96-34-152-30.static.unas.mo.charter.com (96.34.152.30)  39.268 ms  38.911 ms  37.289 ms
11  209.85.244.1 (209.85.244.1)  38.857 ms  38.579 ms  29.242 ms
12  72.14.237.109 (72.14.237.109)  31.330 ms  32.095 ms  27.483 ms
13  ord08s12-in-f23.1e100.net (74.125.225.23)  31.330 ms  38.031 ms  42.130 ms
```

Now, it is time to decipher all the information that is presented. This first command line tells traceroute the parameters that it must use:

```
traceroute to google.ca (74.125.225.23), 30 hops max, 60 byte
packets
```

This gives the hostname, the IP address returned by the DNS server, the maximum number of hops to be taken, and the size of the data packet to be sent. The maximum number of hops can be changed with the -m flag and can be up to 255. In the context of this book, this will not have to be changed.

After the first line, the next few lines show the trip from the BeagleBone, through the intermediate hosts (or hops), to the Google.ca server. Each line follows the following format:

```
hop_number  host_name  (host IP_address)  packet_round_trip_times
```

From the command that was run previously (specifically hop number 4):

```
2   10.149.206.1 (10.149.206.1)   15.335 ms   17.319 ms   17.232 ms
```

Here's a breakdown of the output:

- The hop number 2: This is a count of the number of hosts between this host and the originating host. The higher the number, the greater is the number of computers that the traffic has to go through to reach its destination.
- 10.149.206.1: This denotes the hostname. This is the result of a reverse DNS lookup on the IP address. If no information is returned from the DNS query (as in this case), the IP address of the host is given instead.
- (10.149.206.1): This is the actual host IP address.
- Various numbers: This is the round-trip time for a packet to go from the BeagleBone to the server and back again. These numbers will vary depending on network traffic, and lower is better.

Sometimes, the traceroute will return some asterisks (*). This indicates that the packet has not been acknowledged by the host. If there are consecutive asterisks and the final destination is not reached, then there may be a routing problem. In a local network trace, it most likely is a firewall that is blocking the data packet.

Installing My Traceroute

My Traceroute (**MTR**) is an extension of traceroute, which probes the routers on the path from the packet source and destination, and keeps track of the response times of the hops. It does this repeatedly so that the response times can be averaged.

Now, install mtr with the following command:

```
sudo apt-get install mtr
```

After it is run, `mtr` will provide quite a bit more information to look at, which would look like the following:

```
                        My traceroute  [v0.82]
beaglebone (0.0.0.0)                                    Sat Apr 11 23:14:59 2015
Keys:  Help   Display mode   Restart statistics   Order of fields   quit
                                               Packets              Pings
 Host                                         Loss%   Snt   Last   Avg  Best  Wrst StDev
 1. 192.168.1.1                                0.0%    14    1.5   6.1   1.4  11.8   3.6
 2. 10.149.206.1                               0.0%    14   22.1  16.8   9.6  23.7   4.6
 3. dtr01bxtrmn-tge-0-0-0-3.bxtr.mn.charter.com  0.0%  14   20.9  16.1   9.2  21.3   4.1
 4. dtr01alxnmn-tge-0-1-0-1.alxn.mn.charter.com  0.0%  14   19.6  18.3  11.4  25.6   4.5
    dtr01alxnmn-tge-0-1-0-0.alxn.mn.charter.com
 5. dtr02stcdmn-tge-0-5-0-8.stcd.mn.charter.com  0.0%  14   36.9  23.1  15.0  36.9   6.9
    dtr02stcdmn-tge-0-5-0-10.stcd.mn.charter.com
 6. crr01stcdmn-bue-6.stcd.mn.charter.com       0.0%   14   28.0  27.6  20.4  44.6   7.1
 7. bbr01stcdmn-bue-3.stcd.mn.charter.com       7.1%   14   47.3  31.3  20.2  47.3   9.6
 8. bbr02chcgil-bue-1.chcg.il.charter.com       0.0%   14   39.0  45.3  33.5  70.6  10.6
 9. prr01chcgil-bue-4.chcg.il.charter.com       0.0%   14   36.8  42.6  31.1  63.5   9.4
10. 96-34-152-30.static.unas.mo.charter.com     7.7%   13   33.4  42.3  31.7  63.0  10.0
11. 209.85.244.1                                0.0%   13   35.2  45.4  31.3  81.4  16.7
12. 72.14.237.109                               0.0%   13   33.2  37.1  32.9  43.1   3.3
13. ord08s12-in-f15.1e100.net                   0.0%   13   33.0  36.1  32.0  42.2   3.1
```

While the output may look similar, the big advantage over traceroute is that the output is constantly updated. This allows you to accumulate trends and averages and also see how network performance varies over time.

When using traceroute, there is a possibility that the packets that were sent to each hop happened to make the trip without incident, even in a situation where the route is suffering from intermittent packet loss. The `mtr` utility allows you to monitor this by gathering data over a wider range of time.

Here's an `mtr` trace from my BeagleBone to my Android smartphone:

```
                        My traceroute  [v0.82]
beaglebone (0.0.0.0)                                    Sat Apr 11 23:16:38 2015
Keys:  Help   Display mode   Restart statistics   Order of fields   quit
                                               Packets              Pings
 Host                                         Loss%   Snt   Last   Avg  Best   Wrst  StDev
 1. 192.168.1.2                                0.0%     4   46.4 304.0   6.0  950.2 440.1
```

Here's another trace, after I changed the orientation of the antennae of my router:

```
                        My traceroute  [v0.82]
beaglebone (0.0.0.0)                                    Sat Apr 11 23:17:41 2015
Keys:  Help   Display mode   Restart statistics   Order of fields   quit
                                               Packets              Pings
 Host                                         Loss%   Snt   Last   Avg  Best   Wrst  StDev
 1. 192.168.1.2                                6.7%    15   97.9 189.7   5.0  470.5 164.1
```

As you can see, the original orientation was almost 100 milliseconds faster for ping traffic.

Installing Nmap

Nmap is designed to allow the scanning of networks in order to determine which hosts are up and what services are they offering. Nmap supports a large number of scanning options, which are overkill for what will be done in this book.

Nmap is installed with the following command:

```
sudo apt-get install nmap
```

Answer Yes to install Nmap and its dependent packages.

```
root@beaglebone:~# apt-get install nmap
Reading package lists... Done
Building dependency tree
Reading state information... Done
The following extra packages will be installed:
  fonts-droid fonts-liberation ghostscript gnuplot gnuplot-nox groff gsfonts imagemagick
  imagemagick-common libcups-image2 libdjvulibre-text libdjvulibre21 libexiv2-12 libgs9 libgs9-common
  libijs-0.35 libjbig2dec0 liblcms1 liblensfun-data liblensfun0 liblinear-tools liblinear1
  liblqr-1-0 liblua5.1-0 libmagickcore5 libmagickcore5-extra libmagickwand5 libnetpbm10
  libpaper-utils libpaper1 libsvm-tools libwmf0.2-7 netpbm poppler-data psutils ufraw-batch
Suggested packages:
  ghostscript-cups ghostscript-x hpijs gnuplot-doc imagemagick-doc autotrace cups-bsd lpr lprng
  enscript ffmpeg gimp grads hp2xx html2ps libwmf-bin mplayer povray radiance texlive-base-bin
  transfig xdg-utils exiv2 liblcms-utils liblinear-dev poppler-utils fonts-japanese-mincho
  fonts-ipafont-mincho fonts-japanese-gothic fonts-ipafont-gothic fonts-arphic-ukai
  fonts-arphic-uming fonts-unfonts-core ufraw
The following NEW packages will be installed:
  fonts-droid fonts-liberation ghostscript gnuplot gnuplot-nox groff gsfonts imagemagick
  imagemagick-common libcups-image2 libdjvulibre-text libdjvulibre21 libexiv2-12 libgs9 libgs9-common
  libijs-0.35 libjbig2dec0 liblcms1 liblensfun-data liblensfun0 liblinear-tools liblinear1
  liblqr-1-0 liblua5.1-0 libmagickcore5 libmagickcore5-extra libmagickwand5 libnetpbm10
  libpaper-utils libpaper1 libsvm-tools libwmf0.2-7 netpbm nmap poppler-data psutils ufraw-batch
0 upgraded, 37 newly installed, 0 to remove and 1 not upgraded.
Need to get 29.2 MB of archives.
After this operation, 80.6 MB of additional disk space will be used.
Do you want to continue [Y/n]?
```

Using Nmap

After it is installed, run the following command to see all the hosts that are currently on the network:

```
nmap -T4 -F <your_local_ip_range>
```

The option -T4 sets the timing template to be used, and the -F option is for fast scanning. There are other options that can be used and found via the Nmap manpage.

Here, your_local_ip_range is within the range of addresses assigned by your router.

Here's a node scan of my local network. If you have a lot of devices on your local network, this command may take a long time to complete.

```
root@beaglebone:~# nmap -T4 -F 192.168.1.0-255

Starting Nmap 6.00 ( http://nmap.org ) at 2015-04-11 23:25 UTC
Nmap scan report for 192.168.1.1
Host is up (0.017s latency).
Not shown: 96 closed ports
PORT      STATE SERVICE
53/tcp    open  domain
80/tcp    open  http
548/tcp   open  afp
5000/tcp  open  upnp
MAC Address: C4:04:15:2D:2B:D5 (Unknown)

Nmap scan report for 192.168.1.3
Host is up (0.033s latency).
Not shown: 94 filtered ports
PORT      STATE SERVICE
135/tcp   open  msrpc
139/tcp   open  netbios-ssn
445/tcp   open  microsoft-ds
5357/tcp  open  wsdapi
5800/tcp  open  vnc-http
5900/tcp  open  vnc
MAC Address: 9C:4E:36:8E:46:A4 (Intel Corporate)

Nmap scan report for 192.168.1.5
Host is up (0.0047s latency).
All 100 scanned ports on 192.168.1.5 are closed
MAC Address: 00:11:22:5E:FC:CB (Cimsys)

Nmap scan report for 192.168.1.9
Host is up (0.0055s latency).
Not shown: 97 filtered ports
PORT      STATE SERVICE
135/tcp open  msrpc
139/tcp open  netbios-ssn
445/tcp open  microsoft-ds
MAC Address: 70:5A:B6:15:9C:A4 (Compal Information (kunshan) CO.)
```

Now, I know that I have more nodes on my network, but they don't show up. This is because the command we ran didn't tell Nmap to explicitly query each IP address to see whether the host responds but to query common ports that may be open to traffic.

Instead, only use the -Pn option in the command to tell Nmap to scan all the ports for every address in the range. This will scan more ports on each address to determine whether the host is active or not.

```
root@beaglebone:~# nmap -Pn 192.168.1.0-20

Starting Nmap 6.00 ( http://nmap.org ) at 2015-04-11 23:26 UTC
Nmap scan report for 192.168.1.1
Host is up (0.0038s latency).
Not shown: 994 closed ports
PORT        STATE SERVICE
53/tcp      open  domain
80/tcp      open  http
548/tcp     open  afp
5000/tcp    open  upnp
8200/tcp    open  trivnet1
20005/tcp   open  btx
MAC Address: C4:04:15:2D:2B:D5 (Unknown)

Nmap scan report for 192.168.1.3
Host is up (0.017s latency).
Not shown: 992 filtered ports
PORT        STATE SERVICE
135/tcp  open  msrpc
139/tcp  open  netbios-ssn
445/tcp  open  microsoft-ds
902/tcp  open  iss-realsecure
912/tcp  open  apex-mesh
5357/tcp open  wsdapi
5800/tcp open  vnc-http
5900/tcp open  vnc
MAC Address: 9C:4E:36:8E:46:A4 (Intel Corporate)

Nmap scan report for 192.168.1.9
Host is up (0.0062s latency).
Not shown: 995 filtered ports
PORT        STATE SERVICE
135/tcp    open  msrpc
139/tcp    open  netbios-ssn
445/tcp    open  microsoft-ds
2869/tcp   open  icslap
49167/tcp open  unknown
MAC Address: 70:5A:B6:15:9C:A4 (Compal Information (kunshan) CO.)
```

Here, we can see that there are definitely more hosts registered in the router device table. This scan will attempt to scan a host IP address even if the device is powered off.

Resetting the router and running the same scan will scan the same address range, but it will not return any device names for devices that are not powered at the time of the scan.

You will notice that after scanning, Nmap reports that some IP addresses' ports are closed and some are filtered. Closed ports are usually maintained on the addresses of devices that are locked down by their firewall. Filtered ports are on the addresses that will be handled by the router because there actually isn't a node assigned to these addresses.

Here's a part of the output from an Nmap scan of my Windows machine:

```
root@beaglebone:~# nmap -A -T4 192.168.1.3

Starting Nmap 6.00 ( http://nmap.org ) at 2015-04-11 23:34 UTC
Nmap scan report for 192.168.1.3
Host is up (0.0074s latency).
Not shown: 992 filtered ports
PORT       STATE SERVICE          VERSION
135/tcp   open  msrpc            Microsoft Windows RPC
139/tcp   open  netbios-ssn
445/tcp   open  netbios-ssn
902/tcp   open  ssl/vmware-auth  VMware Authentication Daemon 1.10 (Uses VNC, SOAP)
912/tcp   open  vmware-auth      VMware Authentication Daemon 1.0 (Uses VNC, SOAP)
5357/tcp  open  http             Microsoft HTTPAPI httpd 2.0 (SSDP/UPnP)
|_http-title: Service Unavailable
|_http-methods: No Allow or Public header in OPTIONS response (status code 503)
5800/tcp  open  vnc-http?
5900/tcp  open  vnc              VNC (protocol 3.8)
| vnc-info:
|   Protocol version: 3.8
|   Security types:
|     VNC Authentication
|_    Tight
1 service unrecognized despite returning data. If you know the service/version, please submit the foll
owing fingerprint at http://www.insecure.org/cgi-bin/servicefp-submit.cgi :
SF-Port5800-TCP:V=6.00%I=7%D=4/11%Time=5529AF7A%P=armv7l-unknown-linux-gnu
SF:eabi%r(GetRequest,171,"HTTP/1\.0\x20200\x20OK\r\n\r\n<HTML>\n\x20\x20<H
SF:EAD><TITLE>TightVNC\x20desktop\x20\[beast2\]</TITLE></HEAD>\n\x20\x20<B
SF:ODY>\n\x20\x20\x20\x20<APPLET\x20ARCHIVE=\"tightvnc-jviewer\.jar\"\x20C
SF:ODE=\"com\.glavsoft\.viewer\.Viewer\"\x20WIDTH=1\x20HEIGHT=1>\n\x20\x20
SF:\x20\x20\x20\x20<PARAM\x20NAME=\"PORT\"\x20VALUE=\"5900\">\n\x20\x20\x2
```

Here's a part of the output of a scan of the BeagleBone:

```
root@beaglebone:~# nmap -A -T4 192.168.1.13

Starting Nmap 6.00 ( http://nmap.org ) at 2015-04-11 23:38 UTC
Nmap scan report for 192.168.1.13
Host is up (0.00026s latency).
Not shown: 995 closed ports
PORT       STATE SERVICE          VERSION
22/tcp    open  ssh              OpenSSH 6.0p1 Debian 4+deb7u2 (protocol 2.0)
| ssh-hostkey: 1024 83:54:25:48:68:04:85:b8:e4:cd:27:a9:bc:88:ad:14 (DSA)
|_2048 05:21:e3:4a:84:76:a4:e6:a0:83:33:b7:ff:f0:55:2b (RSA)
80/tcp    open  http?
|_http-methods: No Allow or Public header in OPTIONS response (status code 404)
|_http-title: Bone101
3000/tcp  open  ppp?
3389/tcp  open  ms-wbt-server xrdp
8080/tcp  open  http             Apache httpd 2.2.22 ((Debian))
|_http-title: Index of /
2 services unrecognized despite returning data. If you know the service/version, please submit the fol
lowing fingerprints at http://www.insecure.org/cgi-bin/servicefp-submit.cgi :
==============NEXT SERVICE FINGERPRINT (SUBMIT INDIVIDUALLY)==============
SF-Port80-TCP:V=6.00%I=7%D=4/11%Time=5529B080%P=armv7l-unknown-linux-gnuea
SF:bi%r(GetRequest,B1A,"HTTP/1\.1\x20200\x20OK\r\nX-Powered-By:\x20Express
SF:\r\nAccept-Ranges:\x20bytes\r\nETag:\x20\"2552-1425244362000\"\r\nDate:
SF:\x20Sat,\x2011\x20Apr\x202015\x2023:38:40\x20GMT\r\nCache-Control:\x20p
SF:ublic,\x20max-age=0\r\nLast-Modified:\x20Sun,\x2001\x20Mar\x202015\x202
SF:1:12:42\x20GMT\r\nContent-Type:\x20text/html;\x20charset=UTF-8\r\nConte
SF:nt-Length:\x202552\r\nConnection:\x20close\r\n\r\n---\nlayout:\x20bare\
SF:n---\n<!DOCTYPE\x20html>\n<html>\n\n\x20\x20<head>\n\x20\x20\x20\x20<me
SF:ta\x20charset='utf-8'\x20/>\n\x20\x20\x20\x20<meta\x20http-equiv=\"X-UA
SF:-Compatible\"\x20content=\"chrome=1\"\x20/>\n\x20\x20\x20\x20<meta\x20n
SF:ame=\"description\"\x20content=\"Bone101\x20:\x20Presentation\x20web\x2
```

Installing iptraf-ng

Iptraf-ng is a utility that monitors traffic on any of the interfaces or IP addresses on your network via custom filters. Because iptraf-ng is based on the `ncurses` libraries, we will have to install them first before downloading and compiling the actual iptraf-ng package. To install `ncurses`, run the following command:

```
sudo apt-get install libncurses5-dev
```

Here's how you will install `ncurses` and its dependent packages:

```
root@beaglebone:~# sudo apt-get install libncurses5-dev
Reading package lists... Done
Building dependency tree
Reading state information... Done
The following extra packages will be installed:
  libtinfo-dev
Suggested packages:
  ncurses-doc
The following NEW packages will be installed:
  libncurses5-dev libtinfo-dev
0 upgraded, 2 newly installed, 0 to remove and 1 not upgraded.
Need to get 277 kB of archives.
After this operation, 1038 kB of additional disk space will be used.
Do you want to continue [Y/n]? 
```

Once `ncurses` is installed, download and extract the iptraf-ng **tarball** so that it can be built.

At the time of writing this book, iptrf-ng's version 1.1.4 was available. This will change over time, and a quick search on Google will give you the latest and greatest version to download. You can download this version with the following command:

```
wget https://fedorahosted.org/releases/i/p/iptraf-ng/iptraf-ng-
<current_version_number>.tar.gz
```

The following screenshot shows how to download the iptraf-ng tarball:

```
root@beaglebone:~# wget https://fedorahosted.org/releases/i/p/iptraf-ng/iptraf-ng-1.1.4.tar.gz
--2015-04-11 23:43:47--  https://fedorahosted.org/releases/i/p/iptraf-ng/iptraf-ng-1.1.4.tar.gz
Resolving fedorahosted.org (fedorahosted.org)... 140.211.169.199
Connecting to fedorahosted.org (fedorahosted.org)|140.211.169.199|:443... connected.
HTTP request sent, awaiting response... 200 OK
Length: 583306 (570K) [application/x-gzip]
Saving to: 'iptraf-ng-1.1.4.tar.gz'

100%[====================================>] 583,306     720K/s   in 0.8s

2015-04-11 23:43:57 (720 KB/s) - 'iptraf-ng-1.1.4.tar.gz' saved [583306/583306]
```

After we have completed the downloading, extract the tarball using the following command:

```
tar -xzf iptraf-ng-<current_version_number>.tar.gz
```

Navigate to the iptraf-ng directory created by the `tar` command and issue the following commands:

```
./configure
make
sudo make install
```

After these commands are complete, iptraf-ng is ready to run, using the following command:

```
sudo iptraf-ng
```

When the program starts, you will be presented with the following screen:

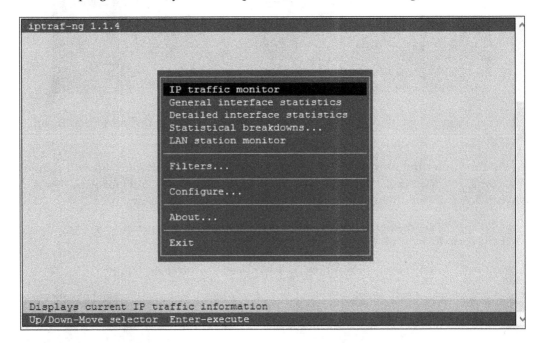

Configuring iptraf-ng

As an example, we are going to monitor all incoming traffic to the BeagleBone. In order to do this, iptraf-ng should be configured.

Selecting the **Configure...** menu item will show you the following screen:

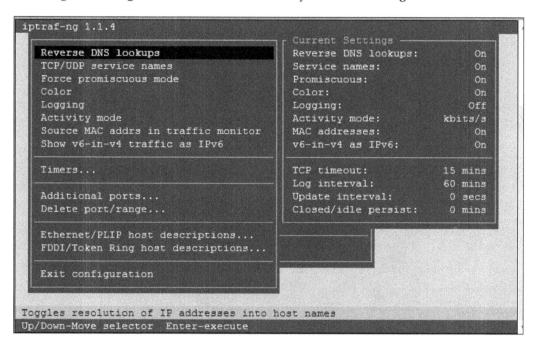

Here, settings can be changed by highlighting an option in the left-hand side window and pressing *Enter* to select a new value, which will be shown in the **Current Settings** window. In this case, I have enabled all the options except **Logging**. Exit the configuration screen and enter the **Filter Status** screen. This is where we will set up the filter to only monitor traffic coming to the BeagleBone and from it.

Then, the following screen will be presented:

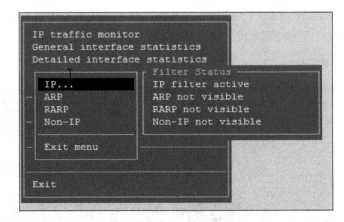

Selecting **IP...** will create an IP filter, and the following subscreen will pop up:

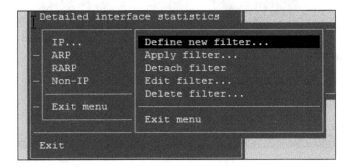

Selecting **Define new filter...** will allow the creation and saving of a filter that will only display traffic for the IP address and the IP protocols that are selected, as shown in the following screenshot:

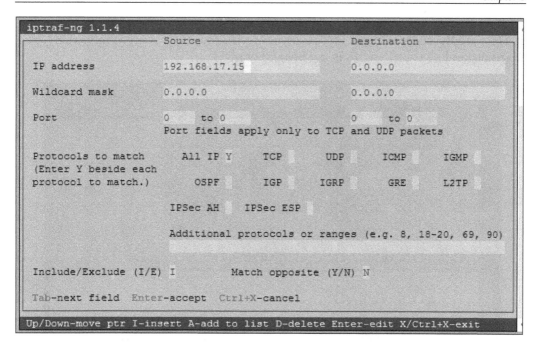

Here, I have put in the BeagleBone's IP address, and to match all IP protocols. Once saved, return to the main menu and select **IP traffic monitor**. Here, you will be able to select the network interfaces to be monitored. Because my BeagleBone is connected to my wired network, I have selected **eth0**. The following screenshot should shows us the options:

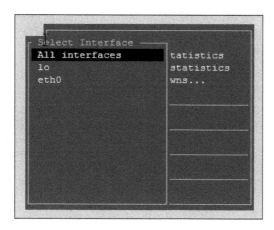

If all went well with your filter, you should see traffic to your BeagleBone and from it. Here are the entries for my PuTTy session; `192.168.17.2` is my Windows 8 machine, and `192.168.17.15` is my BeagleBone:

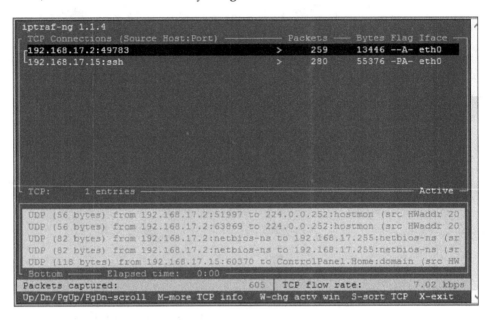

Here's an image of the traffic generated by browsing the DLNA server from the Windows Explorer:

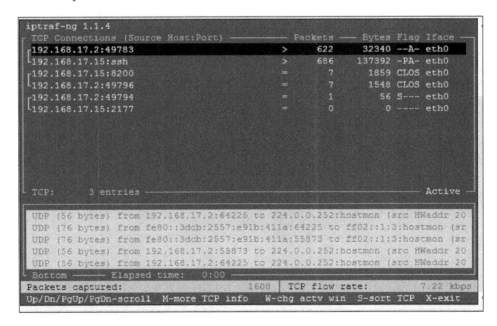

Moreover, here's the traffic from my Android smartphone running a DLNA player, browsing the shared directories that were set up in *Chapter 2, Installing and Configuring Multimedia Server Software*:

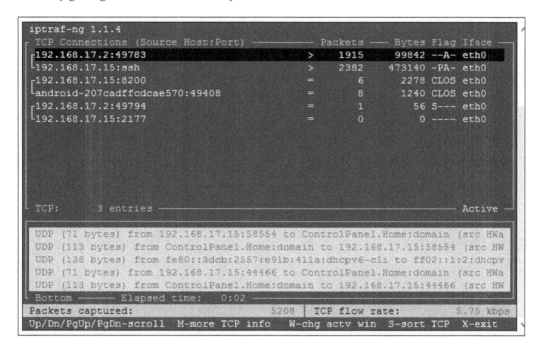

Summary

In this chapter, you saw how to install and configure the software that will be used to monitor the traffic on your local network. With these programs and a bit of experience, you can determine which devices on your network are hogging the bandwidth and find out whether you have any unauthorized users.

In the next chapter, you will see how to add the RAID subsystem to the BeagleBone and how to load it up with content.

4
Installing and Setting Up a BeagleBone RAID System

This chapter will serve as an installation guide for the software that will be used to create a RAID array out of the partitions that you will create on your USB-connected drives. This storage array will then hold all your media files (pictures, videos, and audio) in one drive instead of being spread out over several drives.

For the basics of RAID systems, take a look at `http://en.wikipedia.org/wiki/RAID`.

I don't want to discuss the basics because it is beyond the scope of this book, and other people have done a better job of explaining them than I can ever do. It is, however, important to understand that we will be building a "software" type of RAID array. There are two basic types of RAID arrays (not to be confused with *modes*, as in mode 0, mode 1, and so on).

The first type is called a **hardware RAID**, which as the name suggests, has specialized hardware that makes the array appear as one hard drive to the operating system.

The second type is the type that we will be creating here. This is called a **software RAID** because it uses a software program (`mdadm`) to create a RAID array using discrete drives attached to system.

Determining the available partitions

The first thing that we have to do is to determine the volumes that the Kernel thinks are available to it. We do this using the `fdisk -l` command.

Here's the output of the `fdisk -l` command before you've attached the USB hub and USB disks; the reader should note that only block devices (`mmcblk`) appear in the listing:

```
root@beaglebone:~# fdisk -l

Disk /dev/mmcblk0: 8010 MB, 8010072064 bytes
4 heads, 16 sectors/track, 244448 cylinders, total 15644672 sectors
Units = sectors of 1 * 512 = 512 bytes
Sector size (logical/physical): 512 bytes / 512 bytes
I/O size (minimum/optimal): 512 bytes / 512 bytes
Disk identifier: 0x00000000

        Device Boot      Start         End      Blocks   Id  System
/dev/mmcblk0p1   *        2048      198655       98304    e  W95 FAT16 (LBA)
/dev/mmcblk0p2          198656    15644671     7723008   83  Linux

Disk /dev/mmcblk1: 3925 MB, 3925868544 bytes
4 heads, 16 sectors/track, 119808 cylinders, total 7667712 sectors
Units = sectors of 1 * 512 = 512 bytes
Sector size (logical/physical): 512 bytes / 512 bytes
I/O size (minimum/optimal): 512 bytes / 512 bytes
Disk identifier: 0x00000000

        Device Boot      Start         End      Blocks   Id  System
/dev/mmcblk1p1   *        2048      198655       98304    e  W95 FAT16 (LBA)
/dev/mmcblk1p2          198656     7667711     3734528   83  Linux

Disk /dev/mmcblk1boot1: 1 MB, 1048576 bytes
4 heads, 16 sectors/track, 32 cylinders, total 2048 sectors
Units = sectors of 1 * 512 = 512 bytes
Sector size (logical/physical): 512 bytes / 512 bytes
I/O size (minimum/optimal): 512 bytes / 512 bytes
Disk identifier: 0x00000000

Disk /dev/mmcblk1boot1 doesn't contain a valid partition table

Disk /dev/mmcblk1boot0: 1 MB, 1048576 bytes
4 heads, 16 sectors/track, 32 cylinders, total 2048 sectors
Units = sectors of 1 * 512 = 512 bytes
Sector size (logical/physical): 512 bytes / 512 bytes
I/O size (minimum/optimal): 512 bytes / 512 bytes
Disk identifier: 0x00000000

Disk /dev/mmcblk1boot0 doesn't contain a valid partition table
root@beaglebone:~#
```

If you connect the USB flash drives one at a time to your hub, you can label them as sda and sdb in case they are ever removed.

Moreover, here's the output of the command after you've attached the disks. Note that several new devices have appeared now. Rather that block devices, these devices appear as /dev/sda1 and so on.

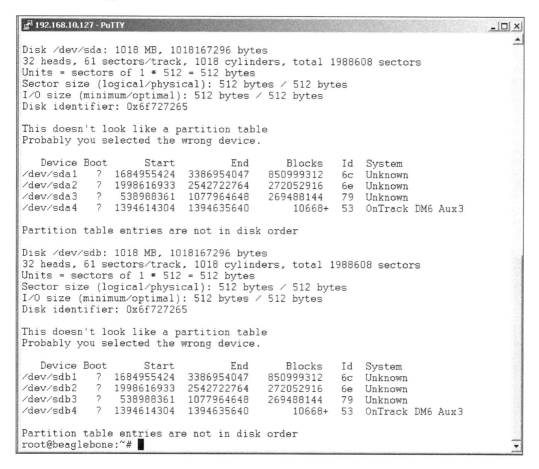

```
192.168.10.127 - PuTTY                                                    _|□|×|

Disk /dev/sda: 1018 MB, 1018167296 bytes
32 heads, 61 sectors/track, 1018 cylinders, total 1988608 sectors
Units = sectors of 1 * 512 = 512 bytes
Sector size (logical/physical): 512 bytes / 512 bytes
I/O size (minimum/optimal): 512 bytes / 512 bytes
Disk identifier: 0x6f727265

This doesn't look like a partition table
Probably you selected the wrong device.

   Device Boot      Start         End      Blocks   Id  System
/dev/sda1    ?   1684955424  3386954047   850999312   6c  Unknown
/dev/sda2    ?   1998616933  2542722764   272052916   6e  Unknown
/dev/sda3    ?    538988361  1077964648   269488144   79  Unknown
/dev/sda4    ?   1394614304  1394635640       10668+  53  OnTrack DM6 Aux3

Partition table entries are not in disk order

Disk /dev/sdb: 1018 MB, 1018167296 bytes
32 heads, 61 sectors/track, 1018 cylinders, total 1988608 sectors
Units = sectors of 1 * 512 = 512 bytes
Sector size (logical/physical): 512 bytes / 512 bytes
I/O size (minimum/optimal): 512 bytes / 512 bytes
Disk identifier: 0x6f727265

This doesn't look like a partition table
Probably you selected the wrong device.

   Device Boot      Start         End      Blocks   Id  System
/dev/sdb1    ?   1684955424  3386954047   850999312   6c  Unknown
/dev/sdb2    ?   1998616933  2542722764   272052916   6e  Unknown
/dev/sdb3    ?    538988361  1077964648   269488144   79  Unknown
/dev/sdb4    ?   1394614304  1394635640       10668+  53  OnTrack DM6 Aux3

Partition table entries are not in disk order
root@beaglebone:~# █
```

 The term *mount* is a leftover from the "good old days" when a techie had to physically mount a disk or magnetic tape on a drive.

If you use the the the `df -k` command, it will show you the filesystems that are mounted and their mount points.

```
192.168.10.107 - PuTTY                                                    _□×
root@beaglebone:~# df -k
Filesystem      1K-blocks     Used Available Use% Mounted on
rootfs            7573112  3185012   4065272  44% /
udev                10240        0     10240   0% /dev
tmpfs              101700     1408    100292   2% /run
/dev/mmcblk0p2    7573112  3185012   4065272  44% /
tmpfs              254248        0    254248   0% /dev/shm
tmpfs              254248        0    254248   0% /sys/fs/cgroup
tmpfs                5120        0      5120   0% /run/lock
tmpfs              102400        0    102400   0% /run/user
/dev/mmcblk0p1      98094    70996     27098  73% /boot/uboot
/dev/mmcblk1p2    3610232   562228   2861280  17% /media/rootfs
/dev/mmcblk1p1      98094    63232     34862  65% /media/BEAGLEBONE
root@beaglebone:~# ▮
```

Preparing the partitions with fdisk

Each partition in the RAID set must be set to the type **Linux raid auto**.

1. We will be doing this using `fdisk` again, as shown in the following screenshot:

```
192.168.10.127 - PuTTY                                                    _□×
root@beaglebone:~# fdisk /dev/sda

Command (m for help): l

 0  Empty            24  NEC DOS          81  Minix / old Lin  bf  Solaris
 1  FAT12            27  Hidden NTFS Win  82  Linux swap / So  c1  DRDOS/sec (FAT-
 2  XENIX root       39  Plan 9           83  Linux            c4  DRDOS/sec (FAT-
 3  XENIX usr        3c  PartitionMagic   84  OS/2 hidden C:   c6  DRDOS/sec (FAT-
 4  FAT16 <32M       40  Venix 80286      85  Linux extended   c7  Syrinx
 5  Extended         41  PPC PReP Boot    86  NTFS volume set  da  Non-FS data
 6  FAT16            42  SFS              87  NTFS volume set  db  CP/M / CTOS / .
 7  HPFS/NTFS/exFAT  4d  QNX4.x           88  Linux plaintext  de  Dell Utility
 8  AIX              4e  QNX4.x 2nd part  8e  Linux LVM        df  BootIt
 9  AIX bootable     4f  QNX4.x 3rd part  93  Amoeba           e1  DOS access
 a  OS/2 Boot Manag  50  OnTrack DM       94  Amoeba BBT       e3  DOS R/O
 b  W95 FAT32        51  OnTrack DM6 Aux  9f  BSD/OS           e4  SpeedStor
 c  W95 FAT32 (LBA)  52  CP/M             a0  IBM Thinkpad hi  eb  BeOS fs
 e  W95 FAT16 (LBA)  53  OnTrack DM6 Aux  a5  FreeBSD          ee  GPT
 f  W95 Ext'd (LBA)  54  OnTrackDM6       a6  OpenBSD          ef  EFI (FAT-12/16/
10  OPUS             55  EZ-Drive         a7  NeXTSTEP         f0  Linux/PA-RISC b
11  Hidden FAT12     56  Golden Bow       a8  Darwin UFS       f1  SpeedStor
12  Compaq diagnost  5c  Priam Edisk      a9  NetBSD           f4  SpeedStor
14  Hidden FAT16 <3  61  SpeedStor        ab  Darwin boot      f2  DOS secondary
16  Hidden FAT16     63  GNU HURD or Sys  af  HFS / HFS+       fb  VMware VMFS
17  Hidden HPFS/NTF  64  Novell Netware   b7  BSDI fs          fc  VMware VMKCORE
18  AST SmartSleep   65  Novell Netware   b8  BSDI swap        fd  Linux raid auto
1b  Hidden W95 FAT3  70  DiskSecure Mult  bb  Boot Wizard hid  fe  LANstep
1c  Hidden W95 FAT3  75  PC/IX            be  Solaris boot     ff  BBT
1e  Hidden W95 FAT1  80  Old Minix

Command (m for help): ▮
```

2. Your disk may come with a number of partitions, as shown here:

```
192.168.10.127 - PuTTY                                              _ |□| x|
root@beaglebone:~# fdisk /dev/sda

Command (m for help): p

Disk /dev/sda: 1018 MB, 1018167296 bytes
32 heads, 61 sectors/track, 1018 cylinders, total 1988608 sectors
Units = sectors of 1 * 512 = 512 bytes
Sector size (logical/physical): 512 bytes / 512 bytes
I/O size (minimum/optimal): 512 bytes / 512 bytes
Disk identifier: 0x6f727265

This doesn't look like a partition table
Probably you selected the wrong device.

   Device Boot      Start         End      Blocks   Id  System
/dev/sda1    ?   1684955424  3386954047   850999312   6c  Unknown
/dev/sda2    ?   1998616933  2542722764   272052916   6e  Unknown
/dev/sda3    ?    538988361  1077964648   269488144   79  Unknown
/dev/sda4    ?   1394614304  1394635640      10668+   53  OnTrack DM6 Aux3

Partition table entries are not in disk order

Command (m for help): █
```

3. First, we must get rid of any existing partitions using the o command,
    as shown in the following screenshot:

```
192.168.10.127 - PuTTY                                              _ |□| x|
Command (m for help): o
Building a new DOS disklabel with disk identifier 0x7685a020.
Changes will remain in memory only, until you decide to write them.
After that, of course, the previous content won't be recoverable.

Warning: invalid flag 0x0000 of partition table 4 will be corrected by w(rite)

Command (m for help): p

Disk /dev/sda: 1018 MB, 1018167296 bytes
32 heads, 61 sectors/track, 1018 cylinders, total 1988608 sectors
Units = sectors of 1 * 512 = 512 bytes
Sector size (logical/physical): 512 bytes / 512 bytes
I/O size (minimum/optimal): 512 bytes / 512 bytes
Disk identifier: 0x7685a020

   Device Boot      Start         End      Blocks   Id  System

Command (m for help): █
```

4. Now that we have removed the unwanted partitions, we can create our own using the n command:

```
192.168.10.127 - PuTTY                                                    _ □ ×

Command (m for help): n
Partition type:
   p    primary (0 primary, 0 extended, 4 free)
   e    extended
Select (default p): p
Partition number (1-4, default 1):
Using default value 1
First sector (2048-1988607, default 2048):
Using default value 2048
Last sector, +sectors or +size{K,M,G} (2048-1988607, default 1988607): 1026047

Command (m for help): n
Partition type:
   p    primary (1 primary, 0 extended, 3 free)
   e    extended
Select (default p): p
Partition number (1-4, default 2):
Using default value 2
First sector (1026048-1988607, default 1026048):
Using default value 1026048
Last sector, +sectors or +size{K,M,G} (1026048-1988607, default 1988607):
Using default value 1988607

Command (m for help): p

Disk /dev/sda: 1018 MB, 1018167296 bytes
32 heads, 61 sectors/track, 1018 cylinders, total 1988608 sectors
Units = sectors of 1 * 512 = 512 bytes
Sector size (logical/physical): 512 bytes / 512 bytes
I/O size (minimum/optimal): 512 bytes / 512 bytes
Disk identifier: 0x0914b259

   Device Boot      Start         End      Blocks   Id  System
/dev/sda1            2048     1026047      512000   83  Linux
/dev/sda2         1026048     1988607      481280   83  Linux

Command (m for help): █
```

5. Select a partition and modify its type using the t command and specify the partition number and type code. Then, use the p command to get the new proposed partition table, as shown here:

```
192.168.10.127 - PuTTY                                                    _ □ ×

Command (m for help): p

Disk /dev/sda: 1018 MB, 1018167296 bytes
32 heads, 61 sectors/track, 1018 cylinders, total 1988608 sectors
Units = sectors of 1 * 512 = 512 bytes
Sector size (logical/physical): 512 bytes / 512 bytes
I/O size (minimum/optimal): 512 bytes / 512 bytes
Disk identifier: 0x0914b259

   Device Boot      Start         End      Blocks   Id  System
/dev/sda1             2048     1026047      512000   83  Linux
/dev/sda2          1026048     1988607      481280   83  Linux

Command (m for help): t
Partition number (1-4): 1
Hex code (type L to list codes): fd
Changed system type of partition 1 to fd (Linux raid autodetect)

Command (m for help): t
Partition number (1-4): 2
Hex code (type L to list codes): fd
Changed system type of partition 2 to fd (Linux raid autodetect)

Command (m for help): p

Disk /dev/sda: 1018 MB, 1018167296 bytes
32 heads, 61 sectors/track, 1018 cylinders, total 1988608 sectors
Units = sectors of 1 * 512 = 512 bytes
Sector size (logical/physical): 512 bytes / 512 bytes
I/O size (minimum/optimal): 512 bytes / 512 bytes
Disk identifier: 0x0914b259

   Device Boot      Start         End      Blocks   Id  System
/dev/sda1             2048     1026047      512000   fd  Linux raid autodetect
/dev/sda2          1026048     1988607      481280   fd  Linux raid autodetect

Command (m for help): █
```

6. Use the w command to permanently save the changes to the /dev/sda disk:

```
192.168.10.127 - PuTTY                                                    _ □ ×

Command (m for help): w
The partition table has been altered!

Calling ioctl() to re-read partition table.

WARNING: Re-reading the partition table failed with error 22: Invalid argument
.
The kernel still uses the old table. The new table will be used at
the next reboot or after you run partprobe(8) or kpartx(8)
Syncing disks.
root@beaglebone:~# █
```

We will not cover the process for the other partitions. It's enough to know that the steps to change the IDs for /dev/sdb1 and /dev/sdb2 are very similar.

Now that we have our RAID drives initialized, it is time to install **Linux Mdadm**, which stands for **Multiple Disk Administrator**.

Installing Mdadm

The first step in the installation of Mdadm is actually the loading of the md module, which the installation software will check for. If it does not find the software, you will get an error message, but Mdadm will definitely not be installed properly.

The following screenshot shows the result of the modprobe md command:

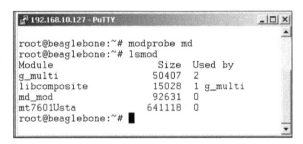

Now that the md module is loaded, the next step in the installation process is to download and install the Mdadm software using the apt command:

apt-get install mdadm

The installation procedure will display the following screens:

That's why we formatted the drives first. This way the installer does all the heavy lifting for us!

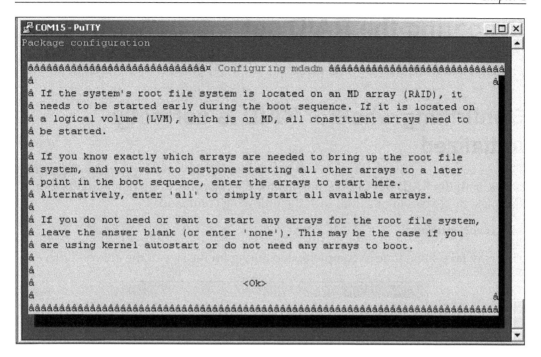

The first thing that the installer will ask you is whether you want to use all the automatically-detected RAID drives in the same array. We want to keep things simple, so we will tell Mdadm to use all the drives we formatted by entering **all**:

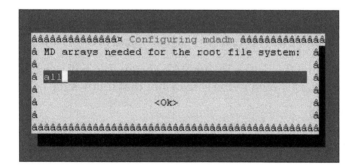

Mdadm will now go off and build our RAID array for us.

Preparing the RAID set

In this section, we will build the actual software RAID drive from our previously prepared and formatted physical drives.

Confirming whether RAID is correctly initialized

The /proc/mdstat file is a dynamically modified log file, which provides the current status of all the RAID devices on the system. We can confirm that the initialization is complete by displaying the file, with the following command:

```
cat /proc/mdstat
```

This may take some time to complete, depending on the size of the attached drives.

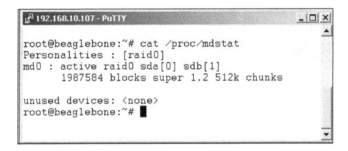

The preceding screenshot shows the result of this command. You will notice that our array is called md0 and that it consists of two physical drives, called sda and sdb.

It's now time to format the drives in our RAID array. We will use the mkfs.ext4 command to do this, as shown in the screenshot that follows the command line:

```
mkfs.ext4 /dev/md0
```

```
192.168.10.107 - PuTTY                                          _ |□| x|
root@beaglebone:~# mkfs.ext4 /dev/md0
mke2fs 1.42.5 (29-Jul-2012)
Filesystem label=
OS type: Linux
Block size=4096 (log=2)
Fragment size=4096 (log=2)
Stride=128 blocks, Stripe width=256 blocks
124416 inodes, 496896 blocks
24844 blocks (5.00%) reserved for the super user
First data block=0
Maximum filesystem blocks=511705088
16 block groups
32768 blocks per group, 32768 fragments per group
7776 inodes per group
Superblock backups stored on blocks:
        32768, 98304, 163840, 229376, 294912

Allocating group tables: done
Writing inode tables: done
Creating journal (8192 blocks): done
Writing superblocks and filesystem accounting information: done

root@beaglebone:~# █
```

Creating the Mdadm.conf configuration file

The new Mdadm installer creates an mdadm.conf file in the /etc/mdadm directory.

All the partitions will be given a UUID label that contains four sets of eight numbers and letters. The mdadm.conf file makes sure that this mapping is remembered when you reboot.

Here, we export the screen's output to create the configuration file by adding a pipe to the mdadm.conf file:

mdadm --detail --scan /dev/md0 > /etc/mdadm.conf

The following screenshot shows the contents of mdadm.conf:

```
192.168.10.107 - PuTTY                                          _ |□| x|
cat mdadm.conf
ARRAY /dev/md0 metadata=1.2 name=beaglebone:0 UUID=f1ba55ee:e2e48a29:c1d343fd:7576ba8f
root@beaglebone:/etc/mdadm# █
```

Creating a mount point for the RAID set

We proceed further by creating a mount point for /dev/md0. In this case, we'll create one called /mnt/raid, which will then be used to store all your media files.

First, we will create a mount point in the /mnt subdirectory of the root file system:

```
mkdir /mnt/raid
```

Then, we will use mdadm to assign this point to /dev/md0:

```
mount /dev/md0 /mnt/raid
```

We then tell mdadm to create the array, as follows:

```
root@beaglebone: mdadm --create --verbose /dev/md0 --level=0 --raid-
devices=2 /dev/sda /dev/sdb
```

This command tells mdadm to create a RAID array called device, md0 and to use our preformatted drives sda and sdb:

```
mdadm: chunk size defaults to 512K
mdadm: /dev/sda appears to be part of a raid array:
       level=raid0 devices=2 ctime=Wed Jan 28 00:44:42 2015
mdadm: partition table exists on /dev/sda but will be lost or
       meaningless after creating array
mdadm: /dev/sdb appears to be part of a raid array:
       level=raid0 devices=2 ctime=Wed Jan 28 00:44:42 2015
mdadm: partition table exists on /dev/sdb but will be lost or
       meaningless after creating array
Continue creating array? y
mdadm: Defaulting to version 1.2 metadata
mdadm: array /dev/md0 started.
```

The command also creates a configuration file called mdadm.conf, which will be used by Mdadm when we reboot, as shown here:

```
root@beaglebone:/etc/mdadm# cat mdadm.conf
ARRAY /dev/md0 metadata=1.2 name=beaglebone:0
UUID=f1ba55ee:e2e48a29:c1d343fd:7576ba8f
```

If you have set up your RAID properly, then enter this command:

```
mdadm --detail --scan /dev/md0
```

This will produce the following output (a properly configured RAID array):

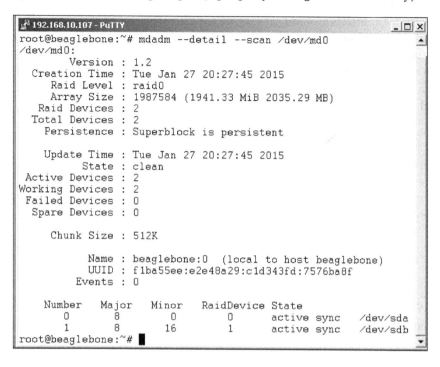

This tells us that the array has been mounted properly on the device md0 and that it is a RAID devices /dev/sda and /dev/sbd. Both these devices are active and synced so that the OS can access both the devices simultaneously (RAID 0).

We then copy some simple text files to the RAID array in order to make sure that it is working. A directory listing is shown in the following screenshot:

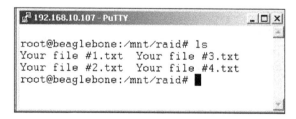

Configuring Samba

Back in *Chapter 2, Installing and Configuring Multimedia Server Software*, when Samba was installed, I told you that you will have to make an entry into the smb.conf file in order to add the RAID array. Now, you can do this so that the RAID array is visible to all the network devices connecting to your BeagleBone. If you have not already done so in *Chapter 2, Installing and Configuring Multimedia Server Software*, edit smb. conf and add the following lines.

```
#Share for the Raid array
[media]
  Comment= Raid array connected to BeagleBone
  path = /media/<Raid mount point>
  read only = no
  browseable = yes
  valid users = <debian>
```

What we are doing here is explained in the following points:

1. We tell Samba the path to the RAID array with the path= statement.

2. We make the directory writeable by telling Samba that it is *NOT* read-only. For security reasons, many Linux settings deny access rather than grant it by default.

3. We then tell Samba which users are allowed to browse the directory. In this case, the default *debian* user. If we had a user called *guest*, we will add them here.

4. You will also have to add the RAID array to the /etc/minidlna.conf so that you can stream your files to any dlna device on your network:

   ```
   #media_dir=/var/lib/minidlna
   port=8200
   media_dir=V,/mnt/raid/Videos
   media_dir=A,/mnt/raid/Music
   media_dir=P,/mnt/raid/Pictures
   friendly_name=Beaglebone DLNA Server
   ```

The functions of these entries are shown in the following screenshot:

```
192.168.10.127 - PuTTY                                              _ |□| x|
# Path to the directory you want scanned for media files.
#
# This option can be specified more than once if you want multiple directories
# scanned.
#
# If you want to restrict a media_dir to a specific content type, you can
# prepend the directory name with a letter representing the type (A, P or V),
# followed by a comma, as so:
#   * "A" for audio    (eg. media_dir=A,/var/lib/minidlna/music)
#   * "P" for pictures (eg. media_dir=P,/var/lib/minidlna/pictures)
#   * "V" for video    (eg. media_dir=V,/var/lib/minidlna/videos)
#
# WARNING: After changing this option, you need to rebuild the database. Either
#          run minidlna with the '-R' option, or delete the 'files.db' file
#          from the db_dir directory (see below).
#          On Debian, you can run, as root, 'service minidlna force-reload' inst
ead.
#media_dir=/var/lib/minidlna
port=8200
media_dir=V,/mnt/raid/Videos
media_dir=A,/mnt/raid/Music
media_dir=P,/mnt/raid/Pictures
friendly_name=Beaglebone DLNA Server
```

Summary

In this chapter, we created a software RAID array using the Mdadm administrator tool, which we downloaded and configured. We then used `fdisk` to set up and format an array of drives.

In the next chapter, we will be setting up a streaming video server using our new RAID array.

5
Streaming Videos

In this chapter, we are going to set up both live and recorded video streaming, using a web-based application. What this means for the user is that they can access either their recorded videos or a live stream from their home IP video camera, from their smartphone, or their tablet while being logged on to their home network.

In order to do this, we have to install some additional software on our BeagleBone. The instructions explained in this chapter are based on an excellent tutorial from HowtoForge:

```
https://www.howtoforge.com/installing-lighttpd-with-php5-php-fpm-and-
mysql-support-on-debian-wheezy
```

Installing MySQL5

The first package that we are going to install is called **MySQL5**.

 All these instructions assume that you have logged in as Root and your network IP address is 192.168.10.127.

To do this, we enter the following command into a terminal (or SSH) window:

```
apt-get install mysql-server mysql-client
```

Once the software has finished installing, the first thing we have to do is set up a root user password.

In the terminal window, enter p. The following message will appear in the window, as shown in the following screenshot:

New password for the MySQL "root" user:

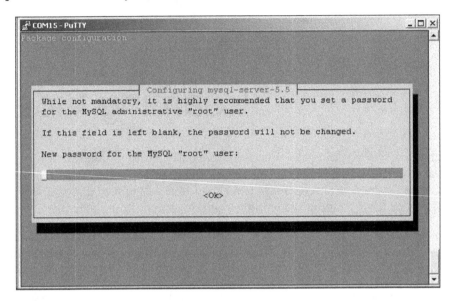

You will then be asked to repeat the password with the following message, as shown here:

Repeat password for the MySQL "root" user:

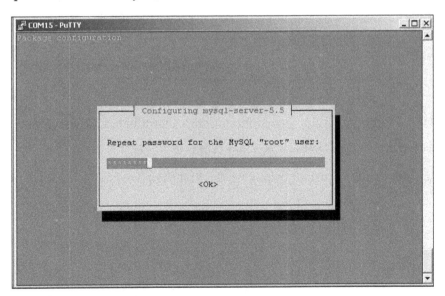

That's it; we are done with MySQL for now.

Installing Lighttpd

The next piece of software that we will be installing is the actual web server software, called **Lighttpd**. This is a server package that has been optimized for embedded applications. It has all the functionality that we will need and consumes relatively few computing resources. For a better reference, refer to `http://www.lighttpd.net/`

> *"With a small memory footprint compared to other web-servers, effective management of the cpu-load, and advanced feature set (FastCGI, SCGI, Auth, Output-Compression, URL-Rewriting and many more) lighttpd is the perfect solution for every server that is suffering load problems. And best of all it's Open Source licensed under the revised BSD license."*

To bring about the installation, we enter the following command in the terminal window:

```
apt-get install lighttpd
```

Disabling Cloud9 services

To prevent the Cloud9 IDE from interfering with your web server, you must disable these services:

```
systemctl disable cloud9.service
systemctl disable bonescript.service
systemctl disable bonescript.socket
systemctl disable bonescript-autorun.service
```

Even with these services disabled, you will still be able to use the Cloud9 IDE to develop code.

If you now enter the IP of the BeagleBone, you will see the Lighttpd placeholder page:

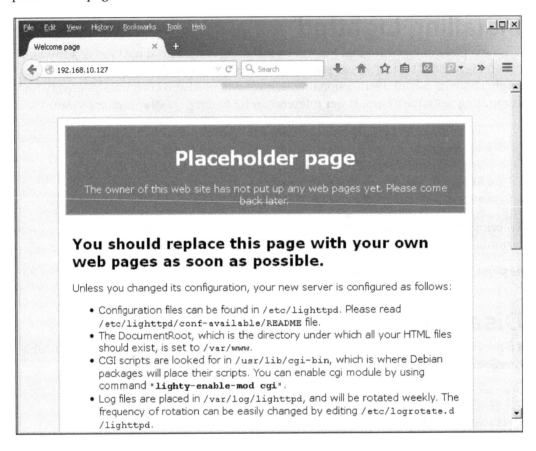

If you get `Error 404`, then you've forgotten to perform `apt-get update` as I suggested. So, you can either do the update now or try using `index.html` instead.

Installing PHP5

Our web-based file browser is a PHP application. Therefore, our next task is to install **PHP5** and **PHP-FPM**. PHP-FPM is a daemon process that runs a **FastCGI** server on port 9000. The `init` script for this application is stored at `/etc/init.d/php5-fpm/php.ini`.

To install these two programs, enter the following command:

```
apt-get install php5-fpm php5
```

Configuring Lighttpd and PHP5

To enable PHP5 in Lighttpd, we must modify `/etc/php5/fpm/php.ini` and uncomment the line `cgi.fix_pathinfo=1`:

```
;http://php.net/cgi.fix-pathinfo
;cgi.fix_pathinfo=1
```

Remove the semicolon present at the beginning of the previous line.

The Lighttpd configuration file for `PHP` `/etc/lighttpd/conf-available/15-fastcgi-php.conf` is suitable for use with `spawn-fcgi`. However, we want to use PHP-FPM; therefore, we create a backup of the file (named `15-fastcgi-php-spawnfcgi.conf`) and modify `15-fastcgi-php.conf`, as follows:

1. `cd /etc/lighttpd/conf-available/`
2. `cp 15-fastcgi-php.conf 15-fastcgi-php-spawnfcgi.conf`
3. `nano 15-fastcgi-php.conf`

We then add the following code to the `config` file:

```
# /usr/share/doc/lighttpd/fastcgi.txt.gz
# http://redmine.lighttpd.net/projects/lighttpd/wiki/Docs:Configuration
Options#mod_fastcgi-fastcgi
## Start an FastCGI server for php (needs the php5-cgi package)
fastcgi.server += ( ".php" =>
        ((
                "socket" => "/var/run/php5-fpm.sock",
                "broken-scriptfilename" => "enable"
        ))
)
```

Lighttpd has a number of different modules that can be enabled by running the `lighttpd-enable-mod <module>` command.

To enable the `fastcgi` configuration, run the following command:

```
lighttpd-enable-mod fastcgi
```

As a result of running the command, the following messages are displayed in the terminal:

```
Available modules: auth accesslog cgi evasive evhost expire fastcgi
flv-streaming no-www proxy rrdtool simple-vhost ssi ssl status userdir
usertrack fastcgi-php-spawnfcgi fastcgi-php debian-doc
Already enabled modules:
Enabling fastcgi: ok
```

```
Run /etc/init.d/lighttpd force-reload to enable changes
```

We proceed further by running the following command:

```
lighttpd-enable-mod fastcgi-php
```

The messages displayed in the terminal will look like the following:

```
Available modules: auth accesslog cgi evasive evhost expire fastcgi
flv-streaming no-www proxy rrdtool simple-vhost ssi ssl status userdir
usertrack fastcgi-php-spawnfcgi fastcgi-php debian-doc
Already enabled modules: fastcgi
Enabling fastcgi-php: ok
```

This creates the `symlinks /etc/lighttpd/conf-enabled/10-fastcgi.conf`, which points to `/etc/lighttpd/conf-available/10-fastcgi.conf`, and `/etc/lighttpd/conf-enabled/15-fastcgi-php.conf`, which points to `/etc/lighttpd/conf-available/15-fastcgi-php.conf`.

Now, enter the following command:

```
cd /etc/lighttpd/conf-enabled
ls -l
```

You will see the following messages in the terminal:

10-fastcgi.conf -> ../conf-available/10-fastcgi.conf

fastcgi-php.conf -> ../conf-available/15-fastcgi-php.conf

We then force a reload, as follows:

```
root@beaglebone: /etc/init.d/lighttpd force-reload
```

This causes the terminal to display the following:

* Reloading web server configuration lighttpd   [OK]

Testing PHP5

The document root of the default website is /var/www. We will now create a small PHP file (info.php) in this directory and call it in a browser:

```
nano Info.php
<?php
phpinfo();
?>
```

The following screenshot shows how `Info.php` looks in a browser:

The file will display lots of useful details about our PHP installation, such as the installed PHP version, as shown here:

PHP5 is working, and it's working through FPM/FastCGI, as shown in the **Server API** line. If you scroll down further, you will see all the modules that are already enabled in PHP5. MySQL is not listed here, which means that we don't have MySQL support in PHP5 yet.

Setting up MySQL support in PHP5

To get MySQL support in PHP, we can install the `php5-mysql` package. It's a good idea to install some other PHP5 modules as well, as you might need them for your applications. You can search for available PHP5 modules as follows:

```
root@beaglebone:/apt-cache search php5
```

You will see the following messages being displayed:

```
php5-curl - CURL module for php5
php5-dbg - Debug symbols for PHP5
php5-dev - Files for PHP5 module development
php5-gd - GD module for php5
php5-gmp - GMP module for php5
php5-ldap - LDAP module for php5
php5-mysql - MySQL module for php5
php5-odbc - ODBC module for php5
```

Pick the modules you need and install them. These are the ones that I installed:

```
apt-get install php5-mysql php5-curl
```

Xcache is a PHP opcode cacher for caching and optimizing PHP intermediate code. Xcache can be installed as follows:

```
apt-get install php5-xcache
```

Reload the PHP-FPM service:

```
/etc/init.d/php5-fpm reload
```

Now, reload `http://192.168.10.127/info.php` in your browser and scroll down to the modules section again.

You should now find lots of new modules here, including the **mysql** module:

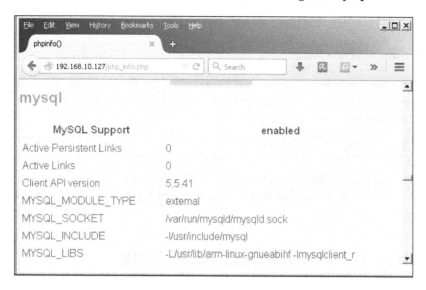

Creating your own home page

Now that we have the required software installed and configured, it is time to install our own software. We will start by installing our home page, called `index.html`, in the directory where Lighttpd expects to find it.

The directory name is `/var/www`, as shown here:

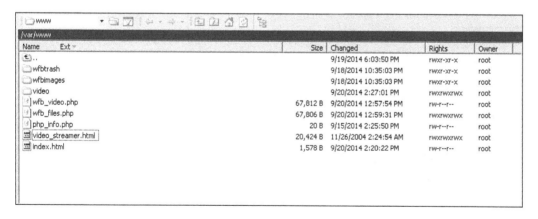

The software uses a modified version of `wfb.php`, which is a web-based file browser written in PHP. It is available for download at `http://cgdave.github.io/webfilebrowser/`.

There are three subdirectories:

- The `wfbtrash` directory is used by `wfb` to store deleted files. This directory must have write privileges enabled or the delete button on the form will not be available.

- The `wfbimages` directory is where the icons for the form are stored. If you want to use your own icons, this is where you will put them.

- The `video` directory is where we will store all our pre-recorded videos. This directory is the cleanest way of keeping our video files separate from the program files.

Creating two modified PHP files

What I have done is created two versions of `wfb.php` and changed the `base directory` information in each file.

The following is the code for `wfb_video.php`:

```
$basedir = "video";// Base directory = custom directory
$filelinks = true;// Links on files enabled
$basevirtualdir = "video" //video directory
```

File links are enabled so that when the user clicks on a given link, the video will automatically start playing, assuming that the required codecs are installed in the browser.

The following is the code for `wfb_files.php`:

```
$basedir = "/";    // Base directory = custom directory
$filelinks = true;// Links on files enabled
$basevirtualdir = "/"; // root directory
```

In this case, the root directory of the file system can be accessed. There doesn't appear to be any way to pass directory information to the PHP code, so we need a different `wfb.php` file for each location.

When the user enters the location of the media server into their browser, they will
be directed to `index.html` on the BeagleBone (in my case, `192.168.10.127`).

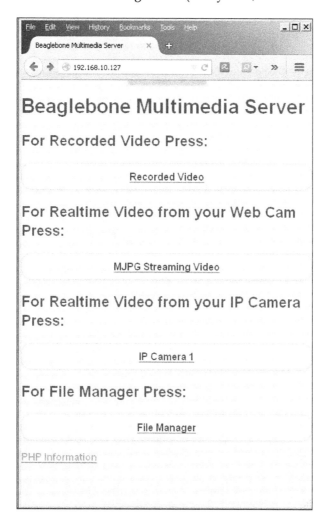

When the user presses the **Recorded Video** button, the following custom file browser screen appears:

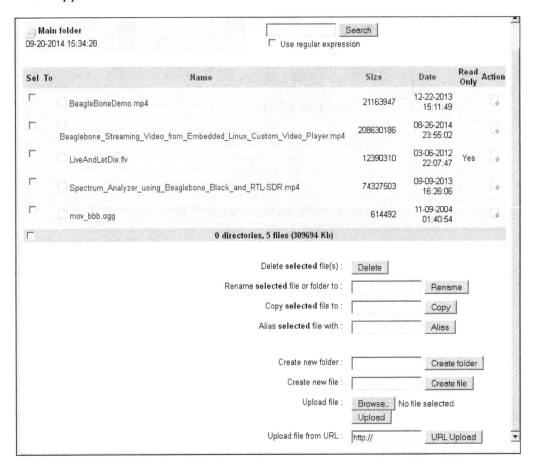

The **File Manager** interface is pretty much the same, except that the browser is now pointing to the root directory of the BeagleBone. This version of the PHP file should have password access enabled in order to keep normal users from damaging things.

As we can see in the following screenshot, we have **Root File System Access**:

In both cases, there is an additional area at the bottom of the page that allows the user to do many of the things that they can do in a graphical user interface based system, including uploading files from the Internet.

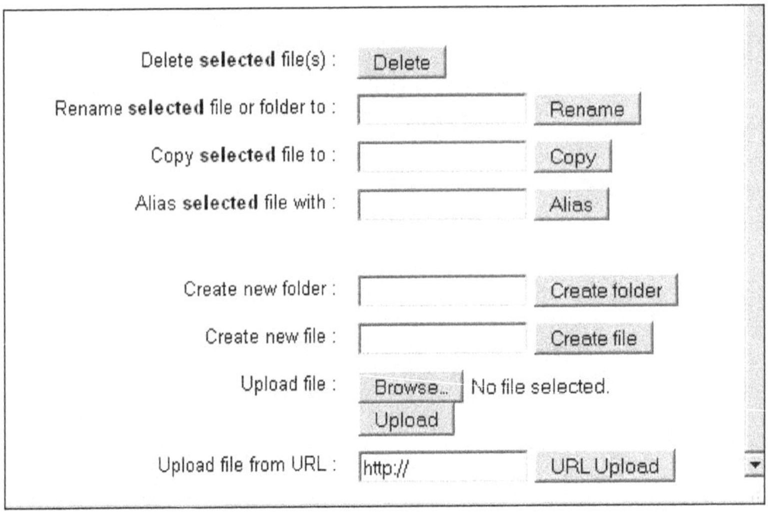

The user is also able to access the IP cameras that are connected to their local network. In this case, the HTML code of index.html must be modified so that it points to the user's camera.

In this case, the IP address is 192.168.10.110 and the default page to view is jview.htm. The reader's IP address and default page will probably be different. This information is for a D-Link DCS-933L camera, which requires the user to log in before accessing the video.

```
<h2>For Realtime Video from your IP Camera Press:</h2>

<p>
<a href="http://192.168.10.110/jview.htm" target="_parent"><button>IP
Camera 1</button></a>
</p>
```

Most, if not all, IP cameras have a built-in web server with a configuration page. What you can *configure* varies from camera to camera, but the most important part is the camera's IP address. In the following screenshot, you will see that I have configured the camera to use a static IP address. This is so that our home page will always be able to find the camera. My network uses the IP addresses 192.168.10. xxx, so I set up the camera at 192.168.10.110 in the LAN settings. My default gateway is 192.168.10.1; yours may be different.

When you access the camera, you must first enter a username and password. The username is `admin` and the password field is blank. You should probably change this in the settings menu.

As you can see in the following screenshot, this particular camera has a number of features that can be **SETUP** for security monitoring:

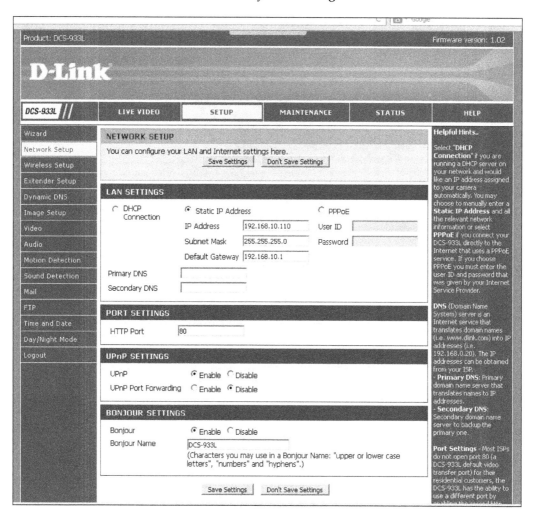

Once this is done, the user can access the camera from the web application by clicking on the **LIVE VIDEO** button at the top of the screen, as shown here:

There are several buttons at the bottom of the video's window, which allows the user to (digitally) zoom in and out, turn the sound on and off, and enable **Night Mode**. In night mode, the camera will automatically detect when the light level drops and will turn on the Infrared LEDs. Other IP cameras will, of course, have different controls, such as pan, tilt, and optical zoom.

Configuring a streaming video

In order to provide video streaming from a USB device in our multimedia setup, we have to first install some software that will allow the BeagleBone to act as a server. The software that I chose to use is called **MJPG Streamer**. If you want to add more functionality than I have here, the instructions are available at `http://shrkey.com/installing-mjpg-streamer-on-beaglebone-black/` and at Sourceforge (`http://sourceforge.net/projects/mjpg-streamer/`).

The first thing we have to do is install the tools and dependencies that we will need to compile the software.

I make it a habit to always do an `apt-get update` to make sure that all the repositories are up to date. The following commands will install the required tools and dependencies. If your tools are already installed and up to date, they will not be overwritten. All the commands assume that you are logged in as root:

1. Run the following command:

    ```
    apt-get install g++ curl pkg-config libv4l-dev libjpeg-dev
    build-essential libssl-dev vim cmake
    ```

2. Then, run this:

    ```
    apt-get install imagemagick
    ```

3. Next, we have to get the code from the website I mentioned earlier:

    ```
    wget https://github.com/shrkey/mjpg-streamer/raw/master
    /mjpg-streamer.tar.gz
    ```

4. Now that we have the tar ball, we can expand it in the directory of our choice:

    ```
    tar -xvf ./mjpg-streamer.tar.gz
    ```

5. The next step is to compile the `mjpg-streamer` code:

    ```
    cd mjpg-streamer


    make USE_LIBV4L2=true


    make install
    ```

6. Now, from the directory that we compiled in, we can run a quick test by typing the following:

    ```
    /mjpg_streamer -i "./input_uvc.so" -o "./output_http.so -w
    ./www"
    ```

This will start the server running from port 8080 of the BeagleBone. The input_uvc.so file is the input device driver used by mjpg_streamer, and output_http.so is the output device driver. The final argument is the directory, where the web page is located, that the video should be sent to.

You will see a screen much like what is shown in the following screenshot; the actual messages shown will depend on the capabilities of your particular camera:

```
MJPG Streamer Version: svn rev:
    i: Using V4L2 device.: /dev/video0
    i: Desired Resolution: 640 x 480
    i: Frames Per Second.: 5
    i: Format...........: MJPEG
    o: www-folder-path...: ./www/
    o: HTTP TCP port.....: 8080
    o: username:password.: disabled
    o: commands..........: enabled
```

If you now go to the web interface described earlier and click on the **Streaming Video** button, you should see the output of your webcam.

The following screenshot is from a cheap dollar store camera (it came with an exercise video for about $3.00):

Summary

In this chapter, we installed and set up our web server software as well as support for PHP scripting and SQL.

We also installed the web page that will allow you to view both recorded video on your file server and live video from IP and USB cameras. The web page also features a web-based file browser, similar to those available with graphical user interfaces.

In the next chapter, we will be setting up a Wi-Fi server so that you can connect to your multimedia server from anywhere within its range.

6
Setting Up a Wireless Access Point

In this chapter, we will be installing and setting up a **Wireless Access Point** (**WAP**) on our BeagleBone system. In the first phase of the installation, our media server will be wide open. Once we have things running smoothly, we will add layers of security.

We will do this by installing and configuring the following programs:

- **hostapd**: This will install the access point software
- **DHCP**: This will provide the user with a local IP address

Installing hostapd

The first thing that we have to do is to make sure that we have the latest version of hostapd, and we can do this with the following commands:

```
apt-get update
apt-get install hostapd
```

```
192.168.10.107 - PuTTY                                          _ |□| x|
root@beaglebone:~# apt-get install hostapd
Reading package lists... Done
Building dependency tree
Reading state information... Done
hostapd is already the newest version.
The following package was automatically installed and is no longer required:
  gdbserver
Use 'apt-get autoremove' to remove it.
0 upgraded, 0 newly installed, 0 to remove and 4 not upgraded.
root@beaglebone:~# ▮
```

As you can see in the previous screenshot, we have the latest version installed.

Now that we know we have the latest version installed, it is time to edit the /etc/default/hostapd configuration file, as follows:

```
nano /etc/default/hostapd
```

We need to add the following line to the file:

```
DAEMON_CONF="/etc/hostapd/hostapd.conf"
```

This is how your hostapd file should look:

```
# Defaults for hostapd initscript
#
# See /usr/share/doc/hostapd/README.Debian for information about
alternative
# methods of managing hostapd.
#
# Uncomment and set DAEMON_CONF to the absolute path of a hostapd
configuration
# file and hostapd will be started during system boot. An example
configuration
# file can be found at
/usr/share/doc/hostapd/examples/hostapd.conf.gz
#
DAEMON_CONF="/etc/hostapd/hostapd.conf" ß Add this line

# Additional daemon options to be appended to hostapd command:-
#    -d    show more debug messages (-dd for even more)
#    -K    include key data in debug messages
#    -t    include timestamps in some debug messages
#
# Note that -B (daemon mode) and -P (pidfile) options are
automatically
# configured by the init.d script and must not be added to
DAEMON_OPTS.
#
#DAEMON_OPTS=""
```

Now that we have referenced the hostapdit, the next file that we have to create is the hostapd.conf file.

You can create and empty the file with the following command:

```
touch /etc/hostapd/hostapd.conf
```

Next, we edit the empty file and add the following text:

```
### Wireless network name ###
interface=wlan0
### Set your bridge name ###
#bridge=br0

#driver
driver=nl80211
country_code=US
## The name of your server##
ssid=Beaglebone Media Server
## Channel to use
channel=7
hw_mode=g
############Security Starts Here#########################
# # Static WPA2 key configuration
# #1=wpa1, 2=wpa2, 3=both
# #wpa=2
## wpa_passphrase=yourpassword
## Key management algorithms ##
## wpa_key_mgmt=WPA-PSK
#
## Set cipher suites (encryption algorithms) ##
## TKIP = Temporal Key Integrity Protocol
## CCMP = AES in Counter mode with CBC-MAC
wpa_pairwise=TKIP
#rsn_pairwise=CCMP
#
## Shared Key Authentication ##
auth_algs=1
## Accept all MAC address ###
macaddr_acl=0
#enables/disables broadcasting the ssid
ignore_broadcast_ssid=0
# Needed for Windows clients
eapol_key_index_workaround=0
```

As I mentioned earlier, security is disabled at this point. At the risk of stating the obvious, a laptop or a tablet with Wi-Fi capability will come in really handy while performing the following steps.

If you turn on your laptop or tablet and "search for available networks," you should see your BeagleBone server on the list. It will be displayed as an **Open** network, because we have not turned on security yet. If you try to connect, your device will say something such as *acquiring a network address* and then hang. This is normal because we haven't set up DHCP yet. We do know, however, that hostapd is alive and well.

Installing DHCP

The **Dynamic Host Control Protocol (DHCP)** is how your computer, tablet, or smartphone gets an IP address when you log on to a network or an access point at your favorite coffee shop.

The first thing to do, once again, is to make sure that we have the latest version of the software installed, with the following commands:

```
apt-get update
apt-get install isc-dhcp-server
```

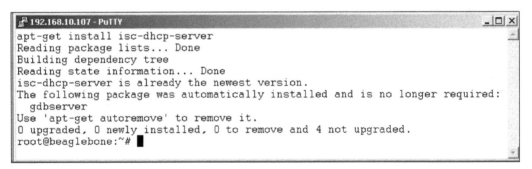

As you can see in the previous screenshot, we have the latest version installed.

Next, we have to edit the configuration file for the DHCP server. For this, we run the following command:

```
nano /etc/dhcp/dhcpd.conf
```

Then, we add the following lines:

```
subnet 192.168.4.0 netmask 255.255.255.0 {
  range 192.168.4.2 192.168.4.10;
}
```

This is how your dhcp.conf file will look:

```
#
# Sample configuration file for ISC dhcpd for Debian
#
#
.
.
.
.
subnet 192.168.4.0 netmask 255.255.255.0 {
  range 192.168.4.2 192.168.4.10;
}
```

Now that we have DHCP configured, we can reboot our BeagleBone and can try to connect to it wirelessly, as shown here:

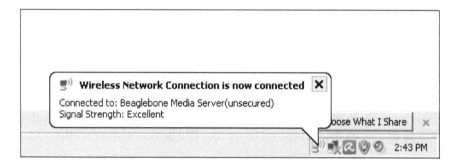

Because we previously installed **Samba**, your media server will also show up in the networks list of your control panel. Depending on your version of Windows, it may look different from the following screenshot:

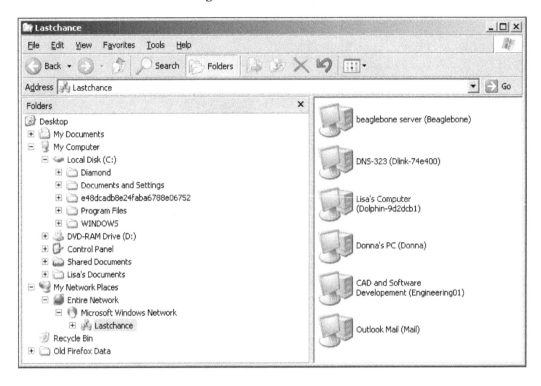

The following screenshot is a screen grab from my Windows XP laptop, which has connected wirelessly to my multimedia server. We can now play music and stream various kinds of videos to the laptop. (Note the IP address shown in the address bar.)

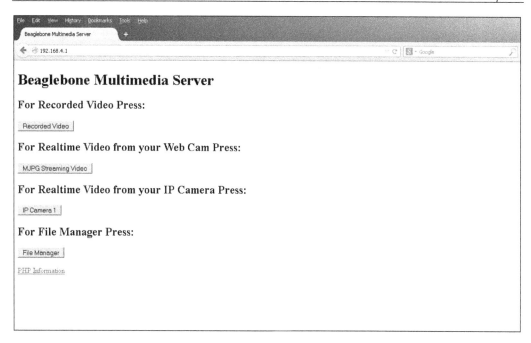

Enabling Wi-Fi security

Now that we have everything up and running, it is time to add some wireless security to our media server. This isn't absolutely necessary, if your server will not be permanently connected to your home network, but I highly recommend that you do it.

The following portion of `hostapd.conf` shows the security part of the file:

```
###########Security Starts Here######################
# # Static WPA2 key configuration
# #1=wpa1, 2=wpa2, 3=both
# #wpa=2
## wpa_passphrase=yourpassword
## Key management algorithms ##
## wpa_key_mgmt=WPA-PSK
```

The first few lines are where we enable WPA/WPA2:

For more information on WEP/WPA/WPA2, just follow
`http://en.wikipedia.org/wiki/Wi-Fi_Protected_Access`.

```
## Set cipher suites (encryption algorithms) ##
## TKIP = Temporal Key Integrity Protocol
## CCMP = AES in Counter mode with CBC-MAC
wpa_pairwise=TKIP
#rsn_pairwise=CCMP
#
## Shared Key Authentication ##
auth_algs=1
```

For information on TKIP, check out `http://en.wikipedia.org/wiki/Temporal_Key_Integrity_Protocol`.

Next, we can set up MAC address filtering:

```
## Accept all MAC address ###
macaddr_acl=0
```

Finally, we can choose to broadcast our SSID.

This option is a bit strange. What we are saying is *don't ignore broadcasting the SSID*; in other words, broadcast the SSID. It is a kind of double negative:

```
#enables/disables broadcasting the ssid
ignore_broadcast_ssid=0
```

```
# Needed for Windows clients
eapol_key_index_workaround=0
```

I will suggest that you enable these features one at a time and check the operation between changes.

The hardware

This is the final section of this chapter and of this book as well. The following is a list of the devices that I used when I was writing this book; I hope you will find them useful:

- **Wi-Fi dongle**: ASUS - WL167G (the following image is an example of it)

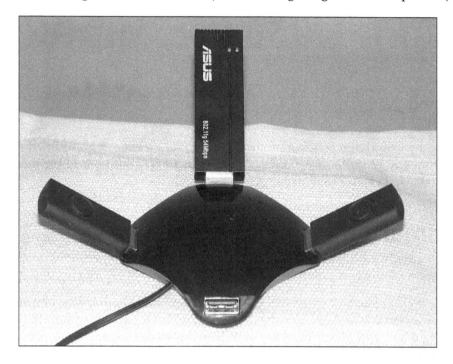

- **USB flash drive**: 8 GB USB Flash drive from Dollarama ($3.00 CDN)
- **Four-port hub**: Targus non-powered from Dollarama ($3.00 CDN) (I will recommend that you use a powered hub if you experience problems or are using a high-power Wi-Fi adapter)

- **12 Volt USB charger**: From Dollarama (~$3.00 CDN)

[*Dollarama* is a local chain store that sells cheap Chinese-made goods for under $5.00]

By using the USB charger shown previously, you can power your multimedia server from any 12 Volt source, such as a car, boat, or RV. With one of the many rechargeable battery packs, you can also take it to the beach.

Summary

In this chapter, we added Wi-Fi connectivity to our multimedia server. You also saw how to secure the access point.

If you have completed all or most of the tasks in the previous chapters, you should now have a portable or fixed multimedia server, which is capable of simultaneously streaming music and MP4 videos to any WiFi-enabled device, any device on your home wired network, or of any other combination.

I hope that this book has been both informative and entertaining and that you enjoy your new multimedia device as much as we enjoyed writing this book.

Index

TKIP
  URL 82
Traceroute
  about 24
  installing 24, 25

V

video streaming
  Cloud9 services, disabling 57
  configuration 71, 72
  home page, creating 63
  Lighttpd, installing 57
  MySQL5, installing 55
  PHP5, installing 58
VNC server
  local time zone, setting 16, 17
  Network Time Protocol (NTP),
      installing 15
  starting 14, 15

W

WAP
  DHCP, installing 78
  hardware 83
  hostapd, installing 75
  setting up 75
w command 45
web file browser
  URL 64
  video directory 64
  wfbimages directory 64
  wfbtrash directory 64
Wireless Access Point. *See* **WAP**

Thank you for buying
Building Networks and Servers Using BeagleBone

About Packt Publishing

Packt, pronounced 'packed', published its first book, *Mastering phpMyAdmin for Effective MySQL Management*, in April 2004, and subsequently continued to specialize in publishing highly focused books on specific technologies and solutions.

Our books and publications share the experiences of your fellow IT professionals in adapting and customizing today's systems, applications, and frameworks. Our solution-based books give you the knowledge and power to customize the software and technologies you're using to get the job done. Packt books are more specific and less general than the IT books you have seen in the past. Our unique business model allows us to bring you more focused information, giving you more of what you need to know, and less of what you don't.

Packt is a modern yet unique publishing company that focuses on producing quality, cutting-edge books for communities of developers, administrators, and newbies alike. For more information, please visit our website at www.packtpub.com.

About Packt Open Source

In 2010, Packt launched two new brands, Packt Open Source and Packt Enterprise, in order to continue its focus on specialization. This book is part of the Packt Open Source brand, home to books published on software built around open source licenses, and offering information to anybody from advanced developers to budding web designers. The Open Source brand also runs Packt's Open Source Royalty Scheme, by which Packt gives a royalty to each open source project about whose software a book is sold.

Writing for Packt

We welcome all inquiries from people who are interested in authoring. Book proposals should be sent to author@packtpub.com. If your book idea is still at an early stage and you would like to discuss it first before writing a formal book proposal, then please contact us; one of our commissioning editors will get in touch with you.

We're not just looking for published authors; if you have strong technical skills but no writing experience, our experienced editors can help you develop a writing career, or simply get some additional reward for your expertise.

BeagleBone Robotic Projects

ISBN: 978-1-78355-932-9   Paperback: 244 pages

Create complex and exciting robotic projects with the BeagleBone Black

1. Get to grips with robotic systems.

2. Communicate with your robot and teach it to detect and respond to its environment.

3. Develop walking, rolling, swimming, and flying robots.

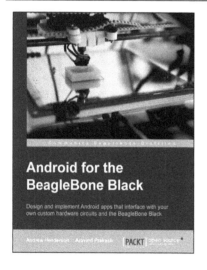

Android for the BeagleBone Black

ISBN: 978-1-78439-216-1   Paperback: 134 pages

Design and implement Android apps that interface with your own custom hardware circuits and the BeagleBone Black

1. Design custom apps that interact with the outside world via BeagleBone Black.

2. Modify Android to recognize, configure, and communicate with sensors, LEDs, memory, and more.

3. A step-by-step guide full of practical Android app examples that will help the users to create Android controlled devices that will use BeagleBone as hardware.

Please check **www.PacktPub.com** for information on our titles

www.ingramcontent.com/pod-product-compliance
Lightning Source LLC
Chambersburg PA
CBHW082122070326
40690CB00049B/4177